Stock Cycles

Stock Cycles

Why Stocks Won't Beat Money
Markets Over the Next Twenty Years

Michael A. Alexander

Writers Club Press
New York   Lincoln   Shanghai

Stock Cycles
Why Stocks Won't Beat Money Markets Over the Next Twenty Years

Writers Club Press
an imprint of iUniverse, Inc.

For information address:
iUniverse
2021 Pine Lake Road, Suite 100
Lincoln, NE 68512
www.iuniverse.com

ISBN: 0-595-13242-1

Printed in the United States of America

Contents

List of Illustrations

List of Tables

Acknowledgements

I would like to acknowledge the contributions of the reviewers of the book: Jim Givens, Jim Janicki, Howard Hill, Walt Oberheu, and Don Roper. I would also like to acknowledge the many useful discussions concerning the Kondratiev cycle by participants of the Longwaves mail list (http//:csf.colorado.edu/forums/longwaves/), especially Eric von Baranov, Bob Bronson, Chris Carolan, Tom Drake, Rich Harriman, Howard Hill and Brian Kavanaugh. Most of all, I wish to thank my wife Kay for her patience and editorial suggestions.

Chapter One

Introduction

Today we hear a lot about the stock market. We are bombarded by advertisements from online brokers and mutual funds. There are countless popular stock market books on the bookstore shelves with more coming every day. Many of them are quite useful; some are not. We are told that stocks go up in the long term; that stocks are the best investment over the long run; and that the best time to invest in stock is always *right now*. There is no doubt that investments in stocks have been very profitable over the last five years. And those who have hesitated because of a belief that stocks are risky have missed out on significant gains.

I find myself skeptical about some of these statements, especially that the best time to invest is always right now. Most who plunked a pile of money into the market just before the 1929-1932 stock market collapse wouldn't agree with that statement. Is it possible they could have anticipated the collapse, considering that the market was grossly overvalued in 1929? Today (January 2000) the valuation on the S&P500 is at unprecedented levels. Some experts maintain that the stock market is in a bubble like 1929 and the market will come crashing down like it did then I should point out that some have been saying this for years and stocks just kept rising. Others say the Internet has transformed the economy, stocks will go much higher and we are on the threshold of a new era for stock investing. Again, many optimists in 1929 believed it was a new era for investing.

How can expert opinions be so diametrically opposed? Can something so important to our financial future as the stock market be so completely unpredictable? Many of us are relying on the stock market to provide for our retirement. Are we relying on the winds of fate for such an important task? There is one thing I have found lacking in the sound and fury of market commentary. Few commentators seem to have much knowledge of what the market has done in the past.

When I first started investing about five years ago, I thought it might be possible to gain some understanding of how the stock market behaves through study of its past behavior. Over the years I have collected historical data on both the stock market and the economy and analyzed this data for patterns of behavior that might repeat in the future. This book describes what I found.

Rather than discussing the behavior of the individual stocks that make up the market, we will be discussing the behavior of a *stock index*. A stock index is simply the average price of a group of stocks. Familiar indices in use today include the Standard and Poor's 500 composite stock index (S&P500), the Dow Jones Industrial Average (DJIA or simply "the Dow") and the National Association of Securities Dealers Automated Quotation (NASDAQ) index. Unless otherwise stated, when discussing stocks in general, or the "stock market" I will be referring to the S&P500 index and its precursors.

Today's investor has the opportunity to invest directly in stock indexes through index funds. A stock index fund is a special mutual fund that is designed to perform the same as a standard stock index, most commonly the S&P500. So when I discuss the decision to be "in stocks" versus "cash", I am referring to investing in an S&P500 index fund versus a money market fund. In general, since most mutual funds underperform the S&P500, the conclusions I reach concerning the index will also apply to most (but not all) mutual funds. The conclusions will also apply to diversified portfolios of large cap stocks, since these stocks make up the S&P500 index.

This book studies the historical behavior of the S&P500 stock index and its predecessors over the last two hundred years. The goal is to use this existing historical record to predict broad trends in stock market performance over the next ten or twenty years. From the historical record, I will present a prediction of investment results that differs substantially from what most investors are being told (and sold) today. I predict that an S&P500 index fund is unlikely to beat a money market return over the next 20 years. I make this prediction using my stock cycle model for long-term market movements.

Chapter two provides strong statistical evidence for a cyclical pattern in the stock market. The historical record (as interpreted by the cycle model) is used to show that there is a 75% probability that the S&P500 index (adjusted for inflation) will be lower twenty years from now than it is today (Jan 2000). With this sort of expected index performance and the low dividends of today, an index fund will most likely underperform money market funds over the next 5-20 years. The same would be true of most mutual funds.

In chapter three we explore the stock cycle model. I present a new valuation tool I developed that can identify where we are in the cycle and whether markets are overvalued or undervalued relative to their long-term prospects. This stock cycle model predicts that the current upwards trend in stock index levels will end, most likely this year (2000) but almost certainly by 2004.

In chapter four I show how long-term shifts in the monetary or the business environment give rise to two *kinds* of stock cycles. A *monetary* cycle occurs when differences in inflation rates produce the up and down portions of the stock cycle. Low inflation is good for stocks (uptrend) and high inflation is bad (downtrend). A *real* cycle occurs when differences in the ability of companies to earn profits produce the up and down portions of the cycle. Strong consistent earnings growth is good for stocks (uptrend), whereas weak, inconsistent earnings growth is bad (downtrend). The current cycle (1966-present) is of the monetary sort, in which the 1966-82 period was the downward portion because of rising inflation, and the period after 1982 has been the upward portion because of falling inflation. The next cycle, which is predicted to begin soon, will be of the real type.

A model is also presented in chapter four to represent these ideas more quantitatively. The model shows that the excellent performance of the S&P500 index in recent years does not reflect a new way of thinking about stocks. Rather it reflects the application of old-fashioned "discount thinking" to the very long economic expansions we have experienced in the 1980's and 1990's. I show that if expansion length were to shorten, as it did during the last downturn in the cycle, a lengthy bear market would be the result. Shorter expansions will make it harder for companies to achieve the sort of sustained profit growth that is necessary to justify continued high stock prices. On the other hand, if economic expansions continue to get longer, the justification for higher and higher stock prices becomes easier and the market should go much higher. Thus, the appearance of the "down" portion of the stock cycle in the near future as predicted by the stock cycle, depends on the appearance of a corresponding "down" portion of the economic cycle. During this "down" period severe recessions would be spaced more closely together than they were during the "up" period. For example, the 1966-1981 "down period" had severe recessions in 1970, 1975 and 1982. In contrast, both the preceding and following "up periods" (1949-66 and 1982-today) had relatively mild recessions spaced further apart.

Stock cycles reflect economic cycles. In chapter five I show that alternating monetary and real stock cycles are a manifestation of an economic cycle called the Kondratiev cycle. Our position within the current Kondratiev cycle is compared with the same position in previous cycles to make a "prediction" of the state of today's economy. At this point in the cycle we should be seeing: 1) the strongest peacetime economic growth in 50 years; 2) mildly rising inflation from a low basis; 3) a strong stock market; 4) the appearance of a vibrant "new economy" within the last decade that is driving the strong growth. This certainly sounds like today.

If this cycle is like previous cycles, what follows should be a lengthy interval of poor long-term stock returns due to poor earnings growth, *not* inflation. This prediction is consistent with the stock cycle model. In chapter six we explore the idea that each Kondratiev cycle creates a "new economy" as it unfolds. The "Internet" or information economy which is the subject of so much hype today is simply the latest new economy. The appearance of the new Internet economy at this point in history strengthens the idea that the Kondratiev cycle is operative and that a lengthy bear market is imminent.

My thesis can be summarized as follows:

1. The Kondratiev cycle produces "new economies" like the current net economy.
2. The Kondratiev cycle creates the stock market cycles as a side effect of the development of the new economy. There are two stock cycles, one monetary and one real, per Kondratiev cycle.
3. Application of Kondratiev cycle analysis to the current economy indicates the start of a long recessionary bear market between 2000 and 2004.
4. This finding agrees with the independent forecast made using my stock cycle model.

In chapter seven I present some of the counter-arguments to my thesis, giving "equal time" to the bulls. By the final chapter the reader will have to decide whether or not the hypothesis is valid. If the reader finds the case for poor returns convincing, chapter eight provides some ideas about investing in a lengthy bear market.

The chapters do not have to be read in order. One can read chapter five and six first to get a feel for the idea of economic cycles. Then one can read the first half of chapter four to see how these cycles cause the stock cycles. Finally one can read chapters 2 and 3 to get predictions of future returns. Or, one can read the chapters in order, and learn about the stock cycles in the order in which I did.

No analyst can give precise answers to questions about the future of the stock market or the economy and be right all the time. This is the realm of prophecy or fortune-telling, not scientific analysis. On the other hand, it is not true that the future is completely unpredictable. As I write this sentence in January 2000 the temperature outside is well below freezing. If you were to ask me to predict whether it will be warmer or colder next Tuesday, I would be unable to give a correct answer. However, if you asked me what sort of temperatures to expect on April 9, I could predict "warmer than today" and almost certainly be right.

You can make this prediction too. How? We can confidently make this prediction because we know that April is a warmer month than January. But what are April and January? They are points in time as marked by our calendar. A calendar is a cyclical model for interpreting time in terms of the seasons. Consider the situation of a farmer. If he plants too early a late frost may destroy his crop. Too late, and he won't get a harvest. It is critical that the farmer properly times his planting with respect to the seasons. In Neolithic times the entire community depended on agriculture, and hence, on the seasonal rhythm of the weather. The entire economy and the livelihood of everyone were determined by seasonality. A model for interpreting time in terms of seasonality that would permit *prediction* of planting times would be incredibly useful information for any Neolithic society. The development of that model, what we now call the calendar, was one of the seminal accomplishments of Man.

Now what precisely *is* the calendar? The calendar is a model of the seasonal cycle that uses the positions of celestial objects to measure the current position in the cycle. It has always been apparent that the length of the day and the seasons are correlated. Days are short in the winter and long in the summer. People discovered that the positions of the sun and stars change with the length of the day and the seasons. By making simple celestial observations ancient peoples were able to measure the length of the seasonal cycle (or year) and found it to be about 365 days long.

The actual length of the year is 365.242199 days, so a 365-day calendar year is about 6 hours too short. The ancients were aware of this and so they constructed calendars in such a way that the average length approached the correct length of the year. In a way calendars represent a measurement of the length of the year. The accuracy of this measurement by pre-modern peoples is quite impressive. Most peoples of antiquity used calendars that implied a length of the year of around 365.25 days. For example, the Julian calendar, upon which our modern calendar is based, used the "leap year" concept in which every fourth year is 366 days long instead of 365 days. This calendar was based on an estimate of exactly 365.25 days for the year, which is 11 minutes too long. Now this seems pretty accurate, but this 11 minute discrepancy adds up over time, making the Julian get ahead of the seasons (what it is supposed to measure) by one day every 130 years. The Julian calendar was introduced in 46 BC. By the sixteenth century it had gotten twelve days ahead of the seasons, which was starting to have an impact on its seasonal timing function. Pope Gregory implemented a new calendar in 1582, which we use today. The Gregorian calendar implies a year of 365.2425 days, which is still 26 seconds too long. The Gregorian calendar represents a measurement of the length of the year to better than one part per million. The ancient Mayan calendar year was even more accurate.

Societies over the millennia have taken their calendars very seriously. They have constructed elaborate observatories (e.g. Stonehenge) for making precise celestial observations in the effort to design accurate calendars. This effort was justified because it was apparent that calendars "worked" to predict the future of an agricultural economy and more accurate calendars worked better. But no one really understood why calendars worked. The most plausible explanation for correlation between the seasonal cycle and the stars was that the gods caused both. The intent of the gods might be interpreted by study of the stars, and the evidence certainly supported this idea. Since the gods controlled the heavens and earth, it was reasonable that they controlled the lives of mere mortals too. Since the will of the gods for the seasons was revealed by the heavens, surely the will of the gods for the insignificant details of a person's life were revealed by the heavens as well. Thus was born the "science" of astrology.

The ancients held both astrology and the calendar as equally valid. Then came Copernicus, Kepler and Galileo, and people discovered *why* there was a linkage between the stars and seasons. The seasons are simply the natural consequence of the fact that the earth revolves around the sun and that the earth's axis of rotation is tilted with respect to the plane defined by the earth's orbit. All of a sudden, it became clear that the calendar "should" work and that it is completely natural that it does. However, this mechanical arrangement of the earth and sun did not provide a mechanism for why astrology should work. Furthermore, the track record of astrology had never been as reliable as the calendar. Deprived the support of the obvious validity of calendrical methods, astrology lost its status as a science.

What we will be working towards in this book is developing a "stock calendar". We wish to develop tools to aid us in the "planting" and "harvest" of our investments and a calendar model seems appropriate. We will see statistical evidence of a cyclical variation in stock Returns, from which we will develop a cyclic model to guide us in future investment decisions.

The purpose of the discussion above was to show how in the absence of many repeated observations, or better yet, a mechanism for a proposed correlation, it is very easy to over-estimate the validity of observed patterns. There is the risk that our stock calendar becomes a type of stock astrology. On the other hand, if the stock cycle can be shown to be highly correlated with other economic cycles the statistical significance of the cycle rises. With this understanding, let us look for patterns in the economy and stock market in order to build our calendar.

Chapter Two

Historical stock market performance

Figure 2.1 shows a plot of the total return that one would have obtained in a hypothetical index fund over the last two centuries. The values are all shown in terms of today's money, that is, the value is adjusted to eliminate the effect of inflation. The value of the investment is shown on a *logarithmic* scale. A fixed distance on this scale corresponds to a fixed percentage gain. Looking at the figure you can see that multiples of ten are spaced equally apart. The straight-line appearance shows that the stock market has tended to give the same percentage return, on average, over the long haul. Since 1802, a stock investment would have grown more than 461,000-fold, equivalent to an average annual return of 6.8% after inflation. This 6.8% real return, when combined with the average inflation rate of 3% during the 20th century, shows that stocks have returned about 10% over the long run. This is far more than the return available on money markets or from bonds. It is this long-term superior performance that prompts financial advisors to recommend stocks over cash or bonds as an investment.

Figure 2.1. Total return on a hypothetical index fund over time (constant dollars)

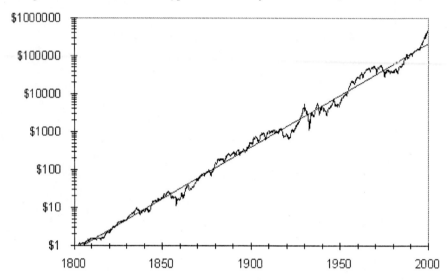

Economist Jeremy Siegel recently wrote an excellent book called *Stocks for the Long Run*, which discusses this long term performance.[1] In fact, the index that I used to describe the long-term performance of the stock market in Figure 2.1 is almost exactly the same as his index (it was constructed with data from the same primary sources). Siegel's conclusions on long-term returns and mine are very similar.

Close examination of Figure 2.1 shows that the actual record does deviate from the trend line. In the context of the entire 200-year trend these deviations seem small, and indeed, the long-term trend does dominate over a sufficiently long time. But none of us is going to live for 200 years. If we restrict our view to shorter periods, there are clearly times, such as the last 20 years, when returns were very good. Similarly, there were periods such as the 16 years before 1982 when returns were rather poor.

It would appear that stocks aren't always the best investments. When I was a teenager in the late 1970's I looked into possibility of investing my college savings in mutual funds to get a better return than from my bank savings account. I went to the library and researched annual returns over the previous ten years. To my surprise, I found that the average mutual fund had returned about 3% over the previous decade, less than a savings account and less than inflation. The very top fund returned less than 12% over that decade (about 6% after inflation). This was hardly impressive.

Stocks have given extraordinary returns since 1982, even with the 1987 stock market crash. Were the 1970's just an anomaly, never to recur? If so, perhaps a stock index fund really is a sure-fire investment. On the other hand, if stocks are guaranteed winners, why is there a debate at all? Could all this good performance over the last 17-18 years be followed by a lengthy period of bad performance? If this is the case, is a stock index fund really the best retirement investment right now?

A statistical treatment of stock returns

Rather than just noting that stocks go up in the long run as shown in Figure 2.1, what we really would like to know is the probability that stock investments made now will continue to be highly profitable. We might be able to gain insight by compiling a list of past returns and recording the frequency at which various returns occurred. To do this, the data in Figure 1 were used to calculate total returns over successive one-year periods starting with January 1802 to January 1803 and ending with December 1998 to December 1999. There are 2359 such periods (the market was closed for four months in 1914). Similarly, total returns were calculated for successive five-year periods starting with January 1802 to January 1807 and ending with December 1994 to December 1999. The same thing was done for ten-year periods and twenty-year periods. The returns for each holding period were ranked in order of return and the values plotted against the percentile frequency in Figure 2.2. Note that Figure 2.2 is scaled to show returns between –10% and +25%. A significant fraction of the one-year returns are outside this range and do not appear in the figure.

Figure 2.2 is interpreted as follows. The vertical axis gives total annualized returns after inflation for various holding periods as a function of probability. On the horizontal axis is the probability that the return will be equal to or better than the value given by the curve. For example, the last five years have shown an average annual return of more than 20%. What is the probability that the next five years will show a real return of 20% or greater? Consulting Figure 2.2, we find the dashed horizontal line representing a 20% return and follow it along until it intersects with the five-year line. The intersection occurs at a percentile value of about 4%. This means there is a 4% chance that we could see five more years of 20% or better returns.

Another interesting exercise is to determine what are the chances of actually losing money to inflation in a stock index fund over the next one, five, ten or twenty years. Proceeding as before, we find the 0% return line and follow it along, noting the percentile values at which each curve is crossed. Over a single year there is a 70% chance of an index fund giving a positive return. By holding for five years, the odds of success rise to 85%. For ten years the odds exceed 90%. Finally, there is a 0% chance of losing money over a 20 year period; a negative real return over a 20 year period has *never* happened in all 2131 such periods over the last 198 years.

A useful way to use this figure is to consider the probability that a stock index investment will outperform a money market. Today (January 2000) money market funds yield about 5%, and the inflation rate is about 2.5%, meaning that money markets are returning about 2.5% after inflation. What we would like to know is how often will this safe 2.5% real return beat the return available from a randomly-placed stock index investment? To do this we consult Figure 2.2 and follow along a 2.5% return line. The intersections give the results: 63% over one year, 74% over 5 years, 82% over ten and 93% over twenty years.

Figure 2.2. Probabilities of various real returns over 1, 5, 10 and 20 year periods

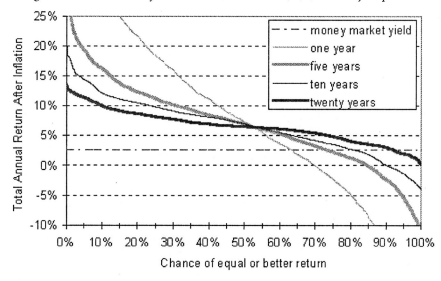

As Figure 2.2 shows, stocks beat money markets most of the time over all the holding periods. The longer the period, the higher the chance of stocks beating money market funds. This is not surprising. The long-term trend in Figure 2.1 becomes more dominant as holding time increases and the return necessarily shifts to the mean. Since this mean is more than twice the money market return, stocks must necessarily beat money markets if they are held long enough. This is why financial advisors urge substantial investments in common stocks. It is also why stock market experts say now is the best time to invest. When they say this they don't mean that by investing now you will get the best return possible, but rather, that the odds of a good return are better with stocks than any other investment.

Is this always true? The assumption behind the above statement is that all periods are alike. Although periods of good and bad performance do occur, they are unpredictable and random, hence your best bet is to go with stocks, especially if you have a long time in which to invest, since the odds improve with holding time. If stock returns are random, we should expect the range of returns depicted in Figure 2.2 to be scattered randomly. That is, in any given time interval we should expect all sorts of returns to occur.

Let us expand on this idea. If stock returns are truly random, then we should expect periods of above and below average performance to appear randomly, like flipping a coin. If we flip fifty coins we should get a result that is fairly close to 25 heads and 25 tails. In general, the farther the outcome is for the average result of 25 heads, the less likely that outcome will be. So while we would see 22 or 27 heads out of fifty coin flips fairly often, we would see 3 or 45 heads very infrequently. The probability of random events like the flipping of fifty coins are described by the binomial distribution. Figure 2.3 shows the binomial distribution for fifty coin flips.

Figure 2.3 Distribution of coin flips and above-average months in a fifty month period.

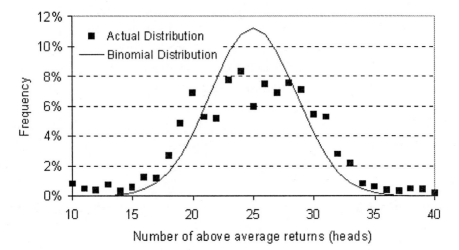

Now let's consider one-month stock index returns as coin flips. We label an above-average return as a "head" and a below-average return as a "tail". We then can represent the returns over a series of fifty months as fifty coin flips. If stock returns are truly random we should expect that the number of above-average returns over this fifty month period to fall into a binomial distribution centered on 25, just as do the number of heads from fifty coin flips. This exercise was performed by calculating 2371 monthly returns using the monthly total return data set for January 1802 to December 1999. For sequential fifty-month periods the number of months with returns higher than the median value was noted. The results were used to construct a frequency distribution of outcomes and plotted in Figure 2.3.

The correspondence is pretty good. The only noticeable difference is that the median outcomes are a little less frequent than predicted and extreme outcomes are somewhat more frequent. This sort of a distribution is called a "fat-tails" distribution since the outliers of the bell-shaped curve (the tail) is bigger than it would be for a purely random phenomenon. Fat tails account for unusual events like stock market crashes, which although rare, are far more common than what would be predicted by a purely random process.

Another way to look at this is to focus on the one-year returns. For example, *each* of the last five years has shown double-digit real returns on the S&P500. Figure 2.2 shows that a better than 10% real return over a one year period occurs about 43% of the time. An occurrence of five double-digit returns in a row should occur about $(0.43)^5$ or 1.5% of the time. This comes to about three times in the last 198 years. Consulting the historical record, we find that five sequential years of double-digit returns occurred in 1924-1929 and 1867-1872, as well as 1994-99. So the excellent recent performance could easily be due to chance and has happened twice before.

So far we have seen that the stock market functions in a fairly random fashion over fairly short periods such as a month or a year. But what about longer periods, like the 1970's when stocks did so poorly, or the 1990's when they have done so well? Do these reflect chance as well, or is there something else at work? We can't perform the same analysis shown in Figure 2.3 for longer periods because we lack sufficient replications. The distribution in Figure 2.3 used monthly data over a fifty-month basis period to obtain one data point. This is the equivalent of flipping each of the fifty coins and then counting the heads. To obtain a reasonably complete distribution, we need to repeat this process many times. Since there are 47 non-overlapping fifty-month periods in the 198-year database, the quality of the data in Figure 2.3 is similar to what would be obtained if we flipped a set of fifty coins 47 times. Now suppose we wanted to look at the frequency of above-average returns during a one-year period. If we wanted to compare the frequency distribution with that for fifty coins, we would have to use a fifty-year basis period. There are, at most, four (largely) non-overlapping fifty-year periods in 198 years. This corresponds to only 4 replications of the coin flips, not enough with which to construct a useful probability distribution.

Table 2.1. *Patterns of above and below average returns for various investment periods*

Period	Pattern of return: above average (H) or below average (T)	No. of periods
20	**THTH TTHH** TH	10
19	**THTH TTHT** HH	10
18	**THTH HHT THTH**	11
17	THHTHHT **HHTT**	11
16	TH **HTHT THTHTH**	12
15	THTTHHH **THTHTH**	13
14	TH **TTHHTT** HTHHTH	14
13	**THTHTHTHTHTH** TTH	15
12	THHHT **HHTT** T **HTHT** TH	16
11	T **HHTTHHTT** T **THTH** HTH	17
10	THH **THTH HTHT THTH** HTTH	19
9	**TTHH** HTHH **HTHT** TH **TTHHTTHH**	22

What we can do is determine whether the returns from successive non-overlapping periods are above or below average. This is equivalent to carrying out a series of coin flips and noting the *sequence* of heads and tails obtained. The sequence is then examined for signs of non-randomness. For example, if we flipped eight coins in sequence and got the result HTHTHTHT, THTHTHTH, TTHHTTHH or HHTTHHTT we would be surprised. Strictly alternating patterns like these are unlikely. The probability of any of these patterns arising from eight random coin flips is 1 in 64. A similar pattern in stock returns from sequential periods would also suggest non-randomness.

Stock returns were calculated over sequential periods 9 to 20 years in length. For each return in sequence it was determined whether it was above (heads) or below (tails) the median value. The results of this assessment were recorded in Table 2.1. For example, consider the first entry for 20 years. There were 10 sequential 20-year periods. The return during the first twenty-year period was below median and so it is marked as a tail (T). The next return was above average and so it is marked as a head (H) and so on to give the sequence THTHTTH-HTH. In each sequence in Table 2.1, special alternating patterns are marked in bold. What we would like to know is whether any of the patterns are sufficiently "special" that its appearance would likely not be the result of chance. In this case, we can surmise that there is some non-random phenomenon that produces these alternating patterns of good and bad returns.

The thirteen year returns show 12 strictly alternating good (H) and bad (T) returns. The probability of such a pattern appearing in *any* of the entries in Table 2.1 is only 3.9%, strongly suggesting that the pattern exhibited by the thirteen-year period is nonrandom. The shortest repeating sequence in the special pattern for the thirteen-year case was two periods long, or 26 years, implying a 26-year cycle might be operating in stock returns. Here we see evidence of non-random behavior on a multi-decade time scale.

None of the other patterns in Table 2.1 show strong evidence of non-randomness. We would expect 1.2 eight-character special patterns purely by chance and there are two. We would expect 5.3 six-character special patterns and there are three. Finally we should expect 22 four-character special patterns and there are seventeen.

Figure 2.4. Sequential thirteen-year returns over time

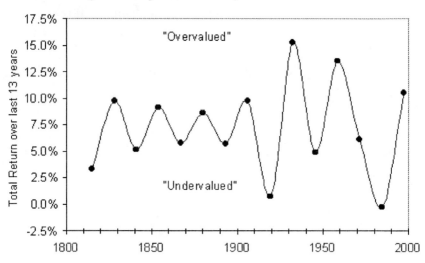

Figure 2.4 shows a plot of these thirteen-year returns. Differences in stock returns, such as the oscillating pattern in Figure 2.4, are caused by changes in stock prices (and hence index values). It has happened on some occasions, such as in 1929-32, that stocks fell a long ways in price, taking a long time to return to their previous levels. Stock market analysts would say that stocks in the period immediately before these price drops were "overvalued". A stock is overvalued when it falls in price afterward and doesn't recover for a long time. Similarly, entire indexes can become overvalued.

Stocks and stock indexes can be undervalued too. If a stock or stock index is undervalued, it will rise in price afterward at a greater than normal rate, and not fall back down. If one buys an index fund when the index is overvalued, the subsequent return will be below average. Conversely, if one buys an index fund when the index is undervalued, the return will be higher than average. So the range of returns shown in Figure 2.2 actually reflect the range of market "valuations" over time, running from very undervalued (high subsequent return) on the left side of the figure to very overvalued (low subsequent return) on the right side. Since returns are, for the most part, randomly distributed, it would seem that market valuation is largely random too, with the exception of the sequence of thirteen-year returns. Figure 2.4 is highly suggestive of a cyclical pattern in the stock market in which the market shifts from overvalued to undervalued and back to overvalued again about every 26 years.

Projection of future returns from overvalued markets

A lot of effort has been put into developing methods of predicting the valuation on the stock market (i.e. an index) because valuation has a big effect on performance. Since one does not know precisely the valuation of the market until after it either falls or rises, what people have done is develop models that correlate with past valuations (which we do know since we have seen what happened afterward). A common valuation tool is the *price to earnings ratio* (P/E) which is the price of a stock or index, divided by its earnings per share. The idea behind P/E is that investors are actually buying an earnings stream when they buy stocks. The value of these earnings (P/E) will then depend on how reliable the earnings stream will be in the future, whether it will grow in the future, and what sort of returns are available from other sorts of investments such as bonds or money markets. In recent years use of the P/E to make investment decisions has fallen out of favor. Many new stocks don't have earnings so a P/E cannot be calculated for them. Also many stocks and indexes that appeared overvalued on the basis of their high P/E rose substantially in price, suggesting that they were actually undervalued. At the same time, presumably undervalued stocks (low P/E) fell in price, suggesting that they were in fact overvalued.

I will present a valuation method in the next chapter that is quite different from the P/E ratio. In this section I use this model to estimate future returns that take into account today's overvalued market. We will see that overvaluation lowers future returns on the S&P500. Although my model was developed using the S&P500, the model is relevant to most stock investments. This is because the vast majority of mutual funds and individual investor portfolios deliver results similar to or worse than the S&P500. So the method is worth considering even for those who manage their own portfolios.

Figure 2.5 shows a new version of Figure 2.2. The returns following the 200 most overvalued months were used to produce Figure 2.5. The stock cycle model was used to pick the 200 months (see chapter three). The idea is that the selection of returns from just overvalued markets (like today) should provide a better idea of the situation facing an investor today than does Figure 2.2, which includes all markets.

Interpretation of Figure 2.5 is the same as for Figure 2.2. Annual returns between −5% and +15% are presented. As with Figure 2.2, a significant fraction of the one-year returns fall outside this range and do not appear in the figure. We can ask the same questions as before, but will get different answers. For example, using Figure 2.2, which includes all market history regardless of valuation, we determined that the chance of a 20% return over the next five years was 4%. Using Figure 2.5, which includes only those markets that have been identified as "overvalued" by my valuation methodology, we find that there is a *zero* chance of the S&P500 index returning even 15% over the next five years.

Figure 2.5. Probabilities of various real returns in "overvalued" markets

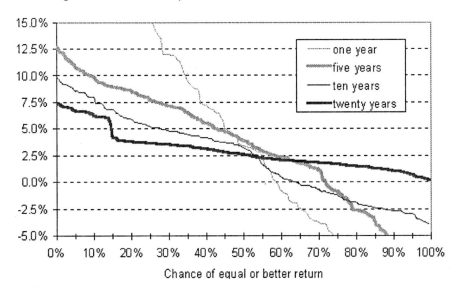

Looking at the chance of loss, we see that the curves start moving down much further to the left than they did in Figure 2.2. Consider the chances of the index beating the 2.5% money market return. Over a one-year period the index beats the money market return 55% of the time in an overvalued market as compared to 62% of the time in all markets. This finding suggests that valuation has little effect on short-term performance, exactly what we would expect for a random process. Over a five-year period, the stock index beats the money market return 58% of the time in overvalued markets as compared to 74% of the time for all markets. Over a ten-year period the index beats the money market return 54% of the time in overvalued markets as compared to 82% of the time in all markets. Finally, over a 20 year period the stock index beats the money rate 52% of the time in overvalued markets compared to 93% of the time in all markets. Notice that holding for longer periods of time does not improve the chances of stock returns beating a money market fund. Overvaluation temporarily suspends the benefits of the long-term upwards trend shown in Figure 2.1. Nevertheless, even in overvalued markets an investment in an index fund still outperforms the money market return more often than not.

The historical returns shown in Figure 2.5 come primarily from dividends, which were a lot higher in the past than they are today. Over the long haul about two-thirds of total return has come from dividends. Today's market shows an extremely low average dividend yield of about 1.2% compared to the historical average of 4.6%. To deal with today's low-dividend market, returns from capital-gains were calculated for the overvalued markets. The results appear in Figure 2.6. To these returns one can add 1-2% for dividends to get an idea of what sort of returns might be forthcoming from today's overvalued, low-dividend market.

Figure 2.6 can be used just like Figures 2.2 and 2.5. For example, what is the chance that the market will be lower (in inflation-adjusted terms) than it is now in one, five, ten or twenty years? A lower market implies a capital-gains return of 0% or less. We find the 0% value on the vertical axis and follow the dashed horizontal line at 0%, noting the probability values when it intersects each of the curves. The 20 year curve was intersected at a probability value of 25%, meaning there is a 25% probability of 0% or better price rise over the next 20 years. This implies a 75% chance of a negative capital gains return over the next twenty years.

Figure 2.6. Probabilities of various real capital gains returns in "overvalued" markets

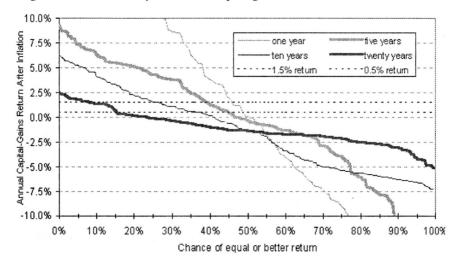

Following along the 0% return line shows probabilities of 35%, 45% and 50% for the index giving a positive real return over the next ten, five and one years. This means there is a 50:50 chance that the market will be lower (in constant dollars) one year from now, which rises to 55% for five years from now, to 65% for ten years from now and to 75% for 20 years from now. Over one year the probabilities are essentially random, yet as the time rises the projected behavior becomes less and less random. Once again the theme of random behavior for the short term and non-random behavior for the long term appears.

To determine the probabilities of stocks beating money markets, we must subtract the low dividend yields of today (1-2%) from the 2.5% real money market return to give a capital gains return of 0.5-1.5%. Note the black dashed lines at 0.5% and 1.5% return lines in Figure 2.6. If we follow these lines along we note that there is only a 9-15% probability of the stock index providing this 0.5-1.5% capital-gains return over the next twenty years. Over ten years the probability rises to 27-38% and over five years it stands at 40-45%. Finally, over a one year period the probability is nearly 50%. Given today's low dividends and high valuations, a money market fund is, on average, a better investment over the next 5-20 years than the S&P500 stock index, or (most likely) a stock mutual fund. In the short term, however, stocks have a good chance of continuing to do well.

The effect of holding time on stock returns in overvalued markets is the opposite of what it is for all markets. Normally, holding stocks for longer amounts of time increases the probability that they will beat other types of investments such as money markets. This observation led to the commonly held belief that for long-term investors, any time is a good time to invest since the long term trend in Figure 2.1 dominates over time. In the case of overvalued markets (like today), holding for longer times, up to twenty years, does *not* increase your odds of success. That is why it is wise today to move assets from large cap stocks, mutual funds and index funds and put them in an alternate investment such as a money market fund.

The reader might rightly question, if returns following overvalued markets are so bad, then how do overvalued markets develop in the first place? One of the things immediately noticeable about stocks and stock indexes is that they move in trends. This trendiness exacerbates the size of moves, making extreme behavior, both positive and negative, more likely than what would be expected for a purely random process. This was shown by the "fat tails" in Figure 2.3. The tendency to move in trends also extends to the longer time frames. Figure 2.1 shows one aspect of long-term trendiness: a rising trend apparent on a time scale of centuries. Figure 2.4 hints at a second aspect of long-term trendiness: a pattern of oscillating upwards and downwards trends that act on a time scale of decades. Stocks will move largely upwards (in constant-dollar terms) for a long time and then abruptly shift to a downward mode. An overvalued market (as defined by the stock cycle model) is one that is close to the time of the shift in trend from up to down.

Conversely, an undervalued market is one that is close to a trend shift from down to up.

The inverse relation between holding time and return relative to cash discussed earlier is a natural consequence of our position in the cycle. Today we are close to the time of trend change from up to down. As we examine projected future returns over longer and longer periods, more and more of that period will fall into the coming downtrend. Hence increasing the holding period of an investment made in an overvalued market fails to improve the performance of that investment compared to money markets. This is why a money market is to be preferred to stocks right now, even though the market may continue to go up for a while longer.

We cannot predict exactly when the next trend shift will occur. If the current uptrend ends in the next year, then one year returns will be bad, if it doesn't then returns will be good. This is shown by the one year return line in Figure 2.6. Returns over the next year have about equal chances of being good or bad.

In the next chapter we will explore the stock cycle model. We will learn of a new valuation tool that can tell you where we are in the cycle and whether markets are overvalued or undervalued relative to their long-term prospects. Based on the stock cycle model, as measured by the valuation tool, the forecast in Figure 2.6 was made. Since the model is cyclic it predicts approximate turning points for the stock market. Specifically, the stock cycle model states that the poor results in Figure 2.6 will be obtained because the current upwards trend in stock index levels will end, most likely this year (2000) but almost certainly by 2004. After it stops going up, the stock index will not go higher (in constant-dollar terms) for a long time, most likely 20 years or more.

Chapter Three

The Stock Cycle

In the last chapter we saw that the expected returns on long-term investments in an index fund can vary widely. Variations in return occur because the market moves in trends that can change in a largely (but not completely) random fashion. The study of price movements on stocks with the idea of predicting future price movements is called *technical analysis*. Although there is a lot of controversy about whether or not technical analysis "works" for short-term predictions, I believe there is little doubt that it works over the longer term. After all, the common observation that "stocks go up in the long run" is itself an application of very long-term technical analysis, based on the expectation that the upwards trend of the past two centuries will continue into the future. In this chapter we will attempt to apply technical analysis over a time scale of decades looking for the cyclical patterns suggested by the analysis in chapter one. Rather than total stock returns we will now be focusing on the stock index, with the effect of dividends excluded.

Secular Market Trends

Charles H. Dow, a founder of the Wall Street Journal and a keen observer of the stock market, is sometimes referred to as the Father of Technical Analysis. Dow identified three time scales of market action: primary, secondary and minor.[2] Primary trends are broad movements that usually last 4-6 years. So long as each rally reaches a higher level than the previous one (or each correction stops at a higher level than the one before) the primary trend is said to be upward and we are in a *bull market*. Conversely, when each intermediate decline carries prices to successively lower levels, or each intervening rally fails to exceed the top of the previous rally, the primary trend is down and we are in a *bear market*. The major advance in the market that started in the beginning of 1995 is an example of a bull market. Secondary trends are the corrections and rallies during bull markets or the declines and counter rallies during bear markets. Normally, they last from a few weeks to a few months. The rally from October 1998 to April 1999 is an example of a secondary trend. The minor trends are short-term movements that usually last less than a week. A host of technical analysis tools have been developed to deal with stock movements at all three time scales.

In this chapter, the idea of *secular* (very long-term) trends is explored. Secular trends consist of one or more primary trends in sequence. As long as each successive bull market high (expressed in constant dollars) is higher than the previous one, we are in a secular bull market. A string of failed bull markets (which fail to rise above the constant-dollar level of a previous bull market), constitutes a secular bear market. The most recent secular bull market began in August 1982. As of early January 2000 it was still in progress. There have been 14 secular trends since 1802: seven secular bull markets and seven secular bear markets.

The impact of secular trends can be discerned by careful examination of the total return plot presented in chapter two (Figure 2.1). A better way to see them is by removing the impact of dividends from the total return. Of the 6.8% total annual real return produced by stocks over the last two centuries, about two-thirds (4.6%) came from dividends. Figure 3.1 shows the total return without the 4.6% return from dividends. This plot shows the long-term real return of 2.2% (6.8% minus 4.6%) that has come as a result of price rise in the index over time. This modified return plot magnifies the subtle deviations from the total return trend that could be seen in Figure 2.1. Inspection of Figure 3.1 clearly shows the secular trends, which have been marked on the figure.

Figure 3.1 can be interpreted as the return due to price increases (and decreases) over time. A secular bear market is a period when prices, in constant-dollar terms, go down (or stay the same) over a significant stretch of time. When the dividend return is added back, the return becomes close to zero. These periods appeared in Figure 2.1 as flat periods, like 1966-1982, the most recent secular bear market. A secular bull market is a time when real prices are rising, so that when the dividend return is added, the total return becomes quite good. These periods show up as the steeply rising portions of the total return plot in Figure 2.1, like 1982-present, the current secular bull market.

Figure 3.1 The dividend-adjusted stock index (in constant dollars) for 1802-1999

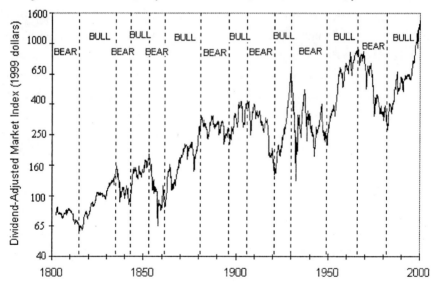

The impact of secular trends on long-term investment performance is very great. To illustrate this, consider two investors, Mr. A and Ms. B. Mr. A is fully invested during the secular bear market periods whereas Ms. B is invested during the secular bull periods (see Table 3.1). All transactions occur in January, so Mr. A bought a hypothetical index fund in January 1802 and sold it in January 1815. Ms. B bought the fund in January 1815 and sold in January 1835, at which point Mr. A bought it again. This continues down until the present. The performance of the two investors is shown in Table 3.1.

Note that despite being invested for 95 years in lengthy chunks of time running from 8-20 years in length, Mr. A's overall return is barely positive in real terms. In contrast, Ms. B gains an average real return of over 13% for her 103 years in the market. Half of the time, such as the last 18 years, index fund investors are in Ms. B's enviable situation. With an average return of more than three times the real interest rate, an index fund is always a better investment during a secular bull market than bonds or money markets. A rational strategy during the secular bull market is then to buy those stocks that are most strongly participating in the bull market, regardless of their price. The faster a stock is rising relative to the average stock (called the relative strength) the more the stock is worth. This observation has given rise to what is called relative-strength or *momentum investing*. The incredible performance of tech stocks (and especially Internet stocks) in recent years can be seen as direct evidence of the popularity of momentum investing. We should expect that momentum methods will remain superior to other investing methods until the end of the secular bull market.

Table 3.1 Performance of investments during secular bear versus bull markets

Mr. A (Secular Bear Markets)			Ms. B (Secular Bull Markets)		
Period	*Duration*	*Real Return*	*Period*	*Duration*	*Real Return*
1802-1815	13	2.8%	1815-1835	20	9.6%
1835-1843	8	-1.1%	1843-1853	10	12.5%
1853-1861	8	-2.8%	1861-1881	20	11.5%
1881-1896	15	3.7%	1896-1906	10	11.5%
1906-1921	15	-1.9%	1921-1929	8	24.8%
1929-1949	20	1.2%	1949-1966	17	14.1%
1966-1982	16	-1.5%	1982-2000	18	14.8%
Overall	**95**	**0.3%**	**Overall**	**103**	**13.2%**

The other half of the time, most recently the 1966-1982 period, investors are in Mr. A's frustrating situation. An index fund under these situations gives a poor return and may actually lose ground to inflation. This was the case in 1966-1982, as I found out in my mutual fund research in 1978. Since the market has little, if any, uptrend during these periods, one might expect that momentum-based investment strategies will fare particularly poorly during these periods. It is the secular trends that cause the wide variation in returns seen over lengthy periods of time like 10 or 20 years. A 10-year period falling completely within a secular bull market will have high returns of 11-15%, whereas one completely within a secular bear market will show close to a zero return. Which return one receives then depends on the timing of the initial investment with respect to the secular bull and market markets. Secular trends also explain why the returns over the last few years have been good despite the high valuations on the stock market. Until the secular bull market ends, the trend is up and high returns will be the norm.

Adjacent secular bear and bull markets define an 18 to 37 year cycle (average 28 years) of stock performance. The returns over the entire cycle tend to be close to the long-term average return on stocks of 6.8% (Table 3.2). The combination of secular bull and secular bear markets largely cancel each other out, leaving the underlying long term trend.

In chapter two we saw evidence for a 26 year-cycle that operated between about 1815 and 1960 (see Figure 2.4). We now see that this apparent 26-year cycle reflected the actual stock cycle shown here. The period of the actual stock cycle is not fixed, but over the period 1815-1960 its length averaged 26.5 years.

P/R, a marker for the stock cycle

In order to define the secular trends/stock cycles; it is useful to express the index value in terms of a parameter that is bounded (restricted to a range of values). An example of such a parameter is the price to earnings multiple or P/E. Stocks go up over time because earnings rise. The ratio P/E does not have to rise for stocks to go up, and P/E will generally remain within a range of values over very long periods of time. By using a bounded parameter like P/E, it should be possible to define stock cycles in terms of cyclical movements in the value of the parameter.

Table 3.2 Historic stock market cycles

Stock Cycle	Cycle Length	Total Real Return		
		Bull Portion	Bear Portion	Entire Cycle
1802-1835	33	9.6%	2.8%	6.9%
1815-1843	28	9.6%	-1.1%	6.4%
1835-1853	18	12.5%	-1.1%	6.0%
1843-1861	18	12.5%	-2.8%	5.2%
1853-1881	28	11.5%	-2.8%	7.2%
1861-1896	35	11.5%	3.7%	8.1%
1881-1906	25	11.5%	3.7%	6.8%
1896-1921	25	11.5%	-1.9%	3.2%
1906-1929	23	24.8%	-1.9%	6.6%
1921-1949	28	24.8%	1.2%	6.5%
1929-1966	37	14.1%	1.2%	7.0%
1949-1982	33	14.1%	-1.5%	6.3%
1966-2000	34	14.8%	-1.5%	6.8%
Average	**28**	**13.2%**	**0.3%**	**6.8%**

Since the cycles we wish to describe are quite long (28 years on average) P/E is not a good choice for this parameter. P/E fluctuates between high and low values more frequently than we would like for a 28-year cycle. The parameter I invented for stock cycles is P/R, the ratio of the index value (P) to business resources (R). Resources are simply the things (plant, equipment, technical knowledge, employee skills, market position etc.) available to the business owner to produce a profit. For a broad-based index, the value of R can be estimated as the sum of retained earnings in constant dollars as given by equation 3.1:

3.1 $\quad R = R_0 + \Sigma rrE_i$

Here rrE_i stands for the *real* retained earnings in year i. That is, it is the difference between what the stocks in the index earned collectively in year i and the dividends paid out in that year, expressed on a constant-dollar basis. R_0 is the value of R in some basis year. For example, R for the S&P500 in fall 1999 was $950. Of this value, $880 represents the sum of rrE for 1999, 1998, 1997 all the way back to 1871 (all expressed in 1999 dollars). The remaining $70 represents the value of R in 1871 (R_0). Details on calculation of R are presented in Appendix A.

The link between business resources (R) and accumulated retained earnings comes from the fact that retained earnings are reinvested in the company in order to grow the business. By growing the business, I mean increasing the ability of the company to make more earnings in the future by increasing the resources (R) available with which to produce earnings. Retained earnings are used to purchase plant and equipment, new product lines, technology, new markets, etc. They create the environment necessary for people to be productive (profitable) workers. Without this environment, no profits could be made and the business would have no value. This environment consists of items, both tangible (office space, machinery, land) and intangible (customer relationships, brand names, managerial systems). The price of these items, like other real things, rises with inflation. This is why we estimate resources by summing previous retained earnings expressed in constant dollar terms.

The underlying meaning of R is subtle. Some resources are physical assets such as plant and equipment, natural resources, or land that can be counted and will show up on a balance sheet. However, most of R resides in the technical and business knowhow of workers. A company in a declining industry provides an environment less conducive to profit generation than a company in a rising industry. The declining firm becomes less able to attract and retain high-caliber employees, and loses R as a result. Companies in rising industries gain increasing numbers of talented employees and gain R. In a way the new employees bring a little R with them when they join a company.

New employees are not blank slates. They can already communicate and process information. Often they already have specialized functions and knowledge bases. That is, they are an asset (they have some R) that produces a return. Now where did they get this R? They got it as part of the cultural transmission they received from the previous generation. The quality of this transmission is a function of the richness of the cultural milieu in which this worker was raised. The richer the milieu, the more R. As a result of the accumulation of past retained earnings, companies grow and pay increasing wages to workers, which makes society richer over time. The richer society provides an ever-improving cultural milieu for the next generation. Hence, successive generations usually have more R than the previous generations. For example, the hard-to-explain tendency for population-average IQ scores to rise over time[3-5] can be interpreted as an effect of increasing R over time.

For example, today's autoworkers and other old-economy workers have reared a generation of computer-savvy children that will be real assets for the companies of the information age. They were able to do this because they worked in an environment (created by decades of accumulated retained earnings in the auto industry) that provided a higher standard of living than their parents had growing up. This higher standard provided a richer cultural experience for their children than the experiences their parents were able to provide. Hence, retained earnings by the auto companies produces R, which shows up in the workers of the next generation. If the car business remains strong they will continue to attract the savvy workers of this generation and will keep the R they created through retained earnings. If not, the young workers will go elsewhere and take the R with them.

So R is not conserved within an individual company. Companies on the rise can pick up "free" R, (i.e. R created by the retained earnings of other companies) while those in declining industries will lose R. On a society-wide basis, as long as there is a rising tide of cultural transmission to new generations, R is conserved. Hence if one looks at a broadly representative index, R should be conserved within the collection of companies inside that index. This is why equation 3.1 "works" for a broad-based index, but not for a narrow index or an individual company. The S&P500 index contains a set of the largest companies that are selected to be representative of the US economy. Collectively, the S&P500 companies carry out a substantial portion of the economic activity in the US. I assume that the S&P500 is sufficiently broad that R is conserved over time and equation 3.1 will give a good estimate for R.

The act of retaining (and investing) profits is what generates new R. This activity puts people to profitable work and increases productivity. Rising productivity produces rising income and a richer culture (more R) that is transmitted to the next generation. Once generated, R exists as part of the culture. It may eventually be used by a wide range of companies other than the ones that originally created the R. Recall that $70 of the $950 of R today ($R_0$ in equation 3.1) existed in 1871. This R_0 was produced by companies before 1871. Almost all of these companies are gone today, but the R they created still lives on as part of the cultural legacy of the past.

Figure 3.2 Business resources (R) versus GDP per capita over time

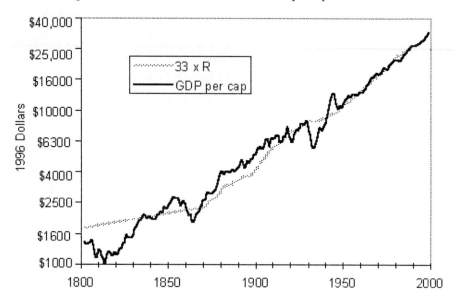

What we are talking about by building up R is economic growth. The high standard of living we enjoy today is our cultural legacy from the investments (R accumulation) made by previous generations, just as the (higher) standard of living that our grandchildren will enjoy will reflect the investments made today. The standard of living can be measured by the real gross domestic product per person (GDP per capita). Figure 3.2 shows a plot of 33 times R versus real per capita GDP. Since the latter part of the nineteenth century R has tracked economic growth quite well. Since 1860 the rate of GDP per capita growth was 1.8% as compared to 1.9% for R. The index before the mid 19th century was comprised of only a handful of stocks, which were hardly representative of the economy as a whole. It is not surprising that R did not track economic growth as well then.

The stock index value is simply a price the market puts on R. All other things being equal, the index should rise at the same rate as R. Figure 3.3 shows that this is indeed the case. From the 1852-3 peak to the market peak in January 2000, the real index has risen at a 2.0% rate, which compares fairly well with 1.9% growth in R and 1.8% growth in GDP per capita over a similar stretch of time. Figure 3.3 shows the value of the raw index in current dollars (unadjusted for inflation) rather than real dollars as shown in Figure 3.1. The value of R was converted into current dollars and plotted in the figure. Finally the ratio of the index (P) to R is shown. Enormous fluctuations in P/R are apparent in the figure. These fluctuations reflect the secular bull and bear market trends. It would appear that the market's opinion of what R is worth changes over time.

A detailed treatment of why these fluctuations in the market's opinion occur is given in chapter four. For now we simply note that the ability to obtain a profit from R varies over time. During favorable economic periods the return from resources (ROR) tends to rise, often producing a secular bull market. There is a limit to ROR, and the secular bull market comes to an end when this limit is reached. This limit is manifested as peaks in P/R. Secular bear markets sometimes reflect periods when ROR is falling. Other times large drops in P/R occur when the value of R rises abruptly due to inflation, temporarily leaving the index behind. This period of lagging P is a secular bear market. Following an inflationary secular bear market, P can rise (eventually) in order to "catch up" with R, or the price of R can fall back to P due to deflation. In either case the result is a secular bull market.

Figure 3.3 Resources (R) compared to the index and P/R

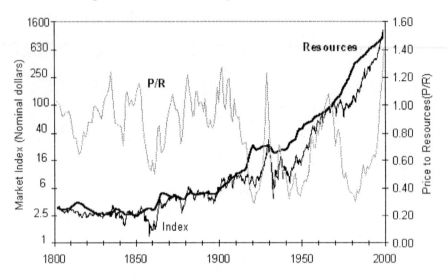

Look at the period around 1815. A sharp rise in the dollar value of R occurred because of inflation. (Recall that Figure 3.3 shows data in terms of current dollars with no adjustment for inflation.) The index did not rise and the result was a drop in P/R signifying a secular bear market (the real value of the index was falling since it failed to rise with inflation). As time went on, price deflation drove the dollar value of R down back to the level of the index and P/R rose, signifying a secular bull market (the real value of the index rose as the dollar became worth more). Now look at the period around 1920. Once again, a sharp rise in the dollar value of R occurred because of inflation and the index did not rise. P/R fell as a result, signifying a secular bear market. This time price deflation did not occur to reduce the dollar value of R back to the level of the index. Instead, after a lag period, the index rose to "catch up" with R. Here we see that stocks, like everything else, rise in price with inflation. The effect is delayed with stocks, however, which is why people don't think of stocks rising because of inflation. The same thing happened in the 1970's, when inflation drove up R, but stocks lagged behind, resulting in a secular bear market. After 1982, stocks started to play catch up with R and by 1996 had done so. In part, the huge bull market since 1982 can be thought of as the (delayed) effect of 1970's price inflation on stock prices.

Figure 3.4 P/R used as a measure of the stock cycle (annual averages)

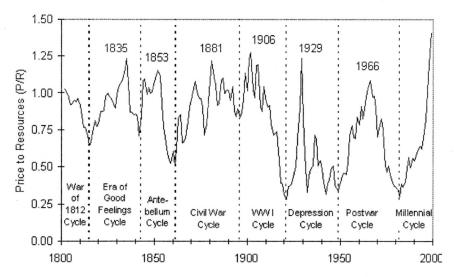

Figure 3.4 shows explicitly how the stock cycles and secular market trends are identified by P/R. With one exception (1906) the secular bull market peaks are defined as peaks in P/R. P/R peaked in 1901, but the index, expressed in constant dollars, reached a higher level in 1906, making 1906 the end of the WW I cycle secular bull market. The rise in the real index value was not as great as the rise in R so P/R fell slightly between 1901 and 1906. Examination of Figure 3.4 shows that the first five secular bull market peaks (1835, 1853, 1881, 1901/6 and 1929) occurred at similar levels of P/R. The 1966 peak was significantly lower than the previous five. The current bull market reached a record level of

P/R in January 1999 and has continued to move higher since then. The high level of P/R today suggests that the current secular bull market is nearing its end.

Market researcher Robert Bronson has identified what he calls Bronson Asset Allocation Cycles[6] or BAACs. The methodology used to determine BAACs is completely different (and more precise) than that used to estimate P/R and detects primary trends (e.g. ordinary bull and bear markets). When coupled with a modified P/E valuation measure,[7] it especially identifies BAAC Supercycles, which appear to be the same thing as secular bull and bear markets. Historically, the BAAC supercycle turning points and those identified by P/R have coincided within a few years of each other. For the S&P500 index, BAAC identified the "asset allocation peak" on April 12, 1999 (this is the date after which investors should start moving out of the S&P500-type stocks and into cash or bonds). This date is consistent with the high level of P/R. Valuation work done by the Yale professor Robert Shiller also supports the idea that the secular bull market already has ended, or will end fairly soon, and that a secular bear market will begin.[8,9]

Use of relative P/R as a fundamental valuation measure

I noted in chapter two that long-standing notions of what a stock is worth, such as P/E, have been swept away in recent years. I mentioned that a new valuation tool was employed to identify overvalued markets that was used to produce the forecasts in Figures 2.5 and 2.6. This tool is P/R. In this section we will see how P/R relates to the key idea of valuation of stocks in terms of their future performance. To start, we will consider what is meant by "value" or, what is a stock worth?

Investors purchase stocks in order to make money. The more money an investor makes from a stock, the more that stock was worth when she bought it. That is, the value of a stock depends on what happens in the future. There are two ways in which an investor can make money from a stock. One is by collecting dividend payments. The other is by selling the stock to someone else at a higher price than what was paid for it. The value of a stock, then, is simply the present value of the two sources of money: future dividends and the proceeds from a future sale of the stock. By present value I mean the quantity of money that, if invested at a particular rate of return called the discount rate, would generate the same amount of money as the stock will. For example, suppose the stock will pay a dividend of $1 next year. To generate this dollar next year we would need to invest ninety-one cents at a 10% rate of return right now. Thus, we say the present value of the $1 dividend next year with a 10% discount rate is $0.91. The present value for a series of n dividend payments made over n years is given by the following formula:

$$3.2 \quad PV_{DIV} = \Sigma \, div_j \cdot (1 + dr)^{-j} \quad for \, j = 1 \, to \, n$$

Here PV_{DIV} refers to the present value of the future dividend stream, div_j is the dividend j years in the future and dr is the discount rate. The present value (PV_S) of the future sale price ($Sale) is the quantity of money invested today at the discount rate of return that will yield the future sale price. It is given by:

$$3.3 \quad PV_S = \$Sale \cdot (1 + dr)^{-j}$$

The value of the stock is the sum of PV_{DIV} and PV_S. These equations are perfectly valid, but not very useful, as they require knowledge of the future price and dividend payments of the stock of interest, which of course, we do not know. We can use these equations to calculate the historical value of stocks (or stock indexes) based on future returns, which we do know for the historical stock index. We can call this quantity the "True Value" (TV) of the historical index based on future returns.

Equations 3.2 and 3.3 were used to calculate TV for the stock index for the period 1802-1969. I chose a rather long period of 30 years for the investment time (n = 30) in order to minimize the effects of the business cycle on dividends and stock prices. $Sale was simply the annual average of the index thirty years in the future. The long-term return on stocks (in constant dollars) over the entire period has been 6.8%. Thus, the discount rate used was 6.8% plus the prevailing inflation rate over the thirty-year investment period. The actual value of the market index was divided by the true value and the resulting ratio plotted in Figure 3.5.

Figure 3.5. The stock index divided by its discounted-future or "true value"

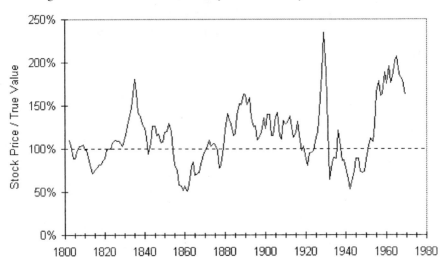

Examination of Figure 3.5 shows that the market rarely prices stocks "right". At times, such as the 1940's, the market underpriced stocks. Long term investments in stocks made at these times will yield average real returns higher than 6.8%. Other times, such as the late 1920's and mid 1960's, the stock market overpriced stocks. Long term investments made during these times will yield average real returns lower than 6.8%. The propensity for the market to over or under price stocks is a consequence of the tendency of the stock market to move in lengthy trends, the secular bull and bear markets. Although this tendency has always been present in the market, it seems to have grown more extreme in the twentieth century as compared to the nineteenth.

A question naturally arises. Is there some way to estimate what the true value of the market is today? To use equations 3.2 and 3.3 directly we would have to wait thirty years to obtain future dividends and stock prices. One way to get around this would be to find a valuation method that can be calculated today that correlates with the true value for historical markets. Figure 3.6 shows P/R plotted along with Price/TrueValue (P/TV). There is a reasonable correlation; peaks and valleys in P/R and P/TV tend to coincide. There is less agreement between the absolute values of P/R and P/TV. P/R was fairly small at the 1960's market peak, yet the market was very overvalued then. We note that the P/R values before and after the 1960's peak were very low, much lower than in the nineteenth century. Relative to the "neighboring" values of P/R, the mid-1960's P/R was quite high. Using a relative value of P/R might be a more effective indicator of value.

Figure 3.6. Price to resources ratio (P/R) compared to price to true value ratio

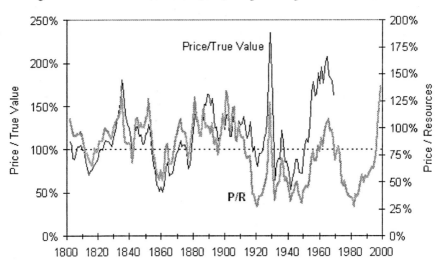

To test this idea, relative P/R values were calculated by dividing current P/R by its average value over the previous cycle. This relative P/R was then plotted along with the price/true value in Figure 3.7. The correspondence between the price to true value and the relative P/R is excellent. Aside from today, the highest value of relative P/R occurred in 1929, when P/TV was also at a maximum. The second highest value of relative P/R occurred in the mid-1960's (when absolute P/R was fairly low). P/TV was at its second highest level then. Both P/R and relative P/R indicate that the price to true value in the early 1980's was probably much less than one, indicating that stocks at that time were underpriced relative to their future 30-year performance. The enormous bull market since then is strong evidence that this was indeed so.

Another interesting observation is to compare the market in 1929 versus 1987. Both years were similar in that a massive bull market driven by disinflation was terminated by a stock market crash. Furthermore, the market was similarly valued in terms of P/E in both years, suggesting an equivalent degree of conventional overvaluation. In terms of relative P/R, the 1929 market was extremely overvalued. In contrast, the 1987 market was *not* overvalued in terms of relative P/R. In actual fact, the 1929 market was extremely overvalued, as shown by the extremely high price to true value. It required 25 years for the market to recover its 1929 highs. The performance of the market since 1987 strongly suggests that the 1987 market was not overvalued like in 1929, although we will not be able to determine a definitive answer to this question until 2017. Nevertheless, had one employed the relative retained earnings as a market value proxy one would have known to sell into the rally following 1929 crash, but to hold after the 1987 crash, which as it turned out, were the correct strategies for the long term investor.

We now come to the 1999 market. The evidence from relative P/R implies that the market today is quite possibly more overvalued relative to future performance than it was in 1929. The determination of some markets as "overvalued" in the previous chapter was made using normalized P/R. The 200 months with the highest normalized P/R in history were used as the sample of "overvalued" markets for Figures 2.5 and 2.6.

Figure 3.7. Relative P/R versus Price / True Value over time

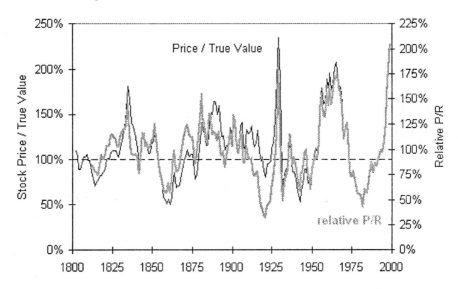

Uses of P/R

Looking at Figure 3.7 it is tempting to conclude that the market is poised to crash just as it did in 1929. Figure 3.4 shows that each time P/R reached values around 1.2-1.3 a secular bear market began. With P/R of around 1.5 today, we must be overdue for a crash. One might be tempted to exploit the coming correction by selling short. [A short sale is when one borrows stock and sells it with the hope of buying it back latter at a cheaper price. It is a bet that the stock is going to go down.] This is not recommended. *P/R is not a useful tool for short-term trading.* For example, had one done this during the sharp correction last summer (P/R hit 1.46 in July and then decreased) he would have lost money in the surprise rally in October 1999.

In the short run, stocks may or may not continue moving higher. The analysis in chapter two shows that the effect of P/R-defined overvaluation historically has been to affect the performance of stock investments over the longer 5-20 year period, not the short-term 1-year period. In the short term, stocks move randomly, overvaluation does not necessarily exert an effect. And so I emphasize, *P/R valuation will not predict precisely when a bear market is going to hit.* What it will predict (assuming historical comparisons are still valid) is that the investment environment will be *much* less favorable over the next decade or two than it was in the last two.

This analysis is sound as long as historical comparisons are still valid. But what if they are not? Suppose this time it *is* different, and the high valuations seen on tech stocks today have become a permanent fixture of the market. We must address this issue before blindly assuming that the simplistic application of historical data expressed as P/R is a valid indicator of future market trends.

The Next Step

In summary, the stock cycle can be measured by the fluctuation of P/R from low to high values as shown in Figure 3.4. P/R was interpreted as the price of a broad market index relative to business resources. The price placed on these resources (i.e. the index value) changes with the market's perception of the ability of management to extract a return from these resources. It is this changing perception that gives rise to the stock cycle. In addition to its role as cycle marker, P/R can be used as a long-range valuation tool. The high value of P/R and the still higher value of relative P/R of today imply that stocks are very overvalued relative to their future performance over the next 30 years.

If we believe that the cycle model is valid, today's market is risky in the extreme. So risky that one marvels at how it could have gotten as high as it has, and why it *still* is going higher. One may rightly question whether the stock cycle is operative in the market today. Although it is clear that the fluctuations that define the stock cycle did occur in the past, how do we know that they will occur again? Perhaps the stock market tends to move in a trend until it abruptly changes course due to an essentially random factor. In this case the observation of a semi-periodic cyclic pattern would be an artifact. All of the statistical data in the last chapter, with a single exception (13 year returns), supported the idea that stock movements are basically random. A market controlled by randomly initiated and terminated stock trends would appear to have moved in a somewhat cyclical fashion in the past, yet a cyclically-based model would have absolutely no predictive power. Without this random factor the trend will continue no matter how high P/R gets.

We really need to understand *why* stock cycles occur in the first place. Without a mechanism, the risk of the stock cycle becoming just another form of stock astrology is too great. Optimally, the mechanism that explains (at least partially) the behavior of the historical stock market should also explain today's market behavior. If a single mechanistic model can explain *both* the secular bull markets of the past and today's extreme bull market, then we will have solid evidence for the validity of the stock cycle model. In the next chapter we will look at some of the drivers behind stock market movements in general. We will find that on a very broad basis, the stock cycle is simply a reflection of an underlying economic cycle. This reflection is not perfect, the stock cycle is not a mirror image of an explicit underlying economic cycle. The translation from the economy to the stock market is subtle and has its own peculiar logic.

Chapter Four

Understanding Stock Market Behavior

In chapter two we learned that stock returns over long periods of time can be quite different depending on when these periods begin. Historically, the market has given lower long-term returns following periods of overvaluation (as defined by P/R) than at other times. In chapter three we learned that the reason for this variation in return was that the market displays long term (secular) trends. Periods of unusually good returns (secular bull markets) alternate with periods of poor performance (secular bear markets). In this chapter we will explore some reasons why the market behaves in this way.

Stock market behavior: effect of monetary conditions

According to Peter Lynch in Fidelity advertisements, we find that stocks go up in the long term because earnings go up in the long term. This is true, but is not the whole story. Figure 4.1 shows the annual average S&P500 index for the periods 1965-1982 (bear) and 1982-1999 (bull) expressed as a ratio to its initial value for each period. Relative annual earnings on the index are also shown in Figure 4.1. Note that earnings grew by about the same amount during both periods, whereas the index performed very differently. Why did almost identical earnings growth produce a 1000% rise in the index during 1982-1999 and no rise during 1965-1982?

The answer is the *monetary environment* was different. Monetary environment refers to the interest rate and inflation rate situation in the economy. Over 1965-1982 inflation averaged about twice its level over 1982-1999. Inflation has a dramatic impact on stock performance because it strongly influences the *perceived value* of a certain amount of earnings. For example, suppose you are considering buying a stock that has provided about $10 per share income over the past five years and it is expected to do the same thing next year. What is this stock worth per share? Suppose there are certificates of deposit (CDs) available that are paying 10% interest. A $100 dollar investment in such a CD would return the same $10 as the stock will, but without risk. So we can say that an upper bound on the value of the stock is $100, since $100 gets you the same return risk-free. Let's say the stock sells at $90 (90% of the CD cost) a price you and other investors collectively are willing to pay for $10 of income.

Now suppose interest rates fell and the CD was paying 5% interest. In this case, you would need $200 to get that $10 of risk-free income. If you could still buy that stock at $90 you certainly would. So would everybody else, and you would find that the stock had risen in price to $180 as interest rates fell. Now the stock hasn't changed, it still pays $10, but the value of the stock in your mind (and everybody else's) has changed because of the change in interest rates.

Now suppose that CDs are paying 5%, but inflation rises to 10%. If you buy the CD, a year from now you will have 5% more dollars, but the total value of your investment in real terms (what it will buy) will have fallen 5%. You would have been better off simply spending the money rather than investing it in the CD. The situation is similar for the stock. If you bought it at $180 you would end up losing money to inflation. Nobody else would be interested in this stock at $180 and so its price would fall to a more reasonable value, probably under $100, in which case one would at least obtain a positive return against inflation. So we see that both interest rates and inflation affect stock prices in an inverse fashion.

One might wonder why I consider inflation and interest rates separately, since they tend to move together. The answer is that this is usually true, but not always. For example, in the late 1940's double digit inflation rates occurred at the same time as 1% interest rates, and bank accounts in the late 1970's yielded less than inflation. In today's market we need only watch interest rates, but in the past, stock prices have reflected inflation even when interest rates have not.

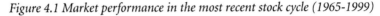

Figure 4.1 Market performance in the most recent stock cycle (1965-1999)

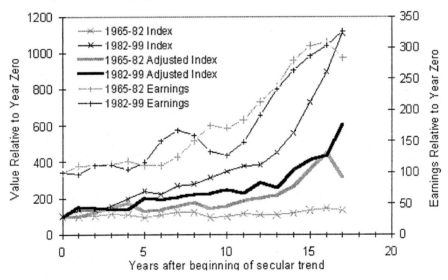

Let us define the *effective interest rate* (EI) as the larger of the interest rate or inflation rate. EI captures the effects of both inflation and interest rates in a single variable. Using this parameter we can say that a stock that sells at $10 per dollar of earnings, (P/E of 10) in a monetary environment typified by a 10% EI is valued the same as a stock selling for a P/E of 20 in a monetary environment characterized by an EI of 5%. We can define a monetarily adjusted index as follows:

4.1   adjusted index = regular index • (EI / EI at year 0)

This adjusted index removes the effects of monetary environment. Consider our stock example from above. Let's say in year zero interest rates are 10% with low inflation (EI = 10%) and the stock sells at $90. The next year interest rates fall to 5% with low inflation (EI = 5%) and the stock sells for $180. One year later, interest rates are still 5%, but inflation has now risen to 10% (EI = 10%) and the stock sells at $90. If we apply equation 4.1 to calculate an adjusted stock price for each year we obtain a value of $90 for all three years. The adjusted value didn't change at all, despite the wild fluctuations in the regular price. This makes sense since what you get for owning the stock ($10 of income) hasn't changed.

Equation 4.1 was applied to the index plots in Figure 4.1 to obtain monetary-adjusted indexes. These appear as the bold lines. Note that the adjusted indexes from the 1965-1982 and 1982-1999 periods show similar profiles, just as the earnings do. Once the effect of the monetary environment is removed, we see that the adjusted value of the index rose by about the same amount over the two periods. Since the value of stocks ultimately derive from their earnings, it makes perfect sense for the adjusted value to follow earnings growth. So Peter Lynch is right about earnings, but with a twist. We now see that the major difference between the poor performance in the 1970's and the good performance in the 1990's is the monetary environment (as characterized by EI). The 1970's had a rising EI, which suppressed stock price growth, the 1990's had a falling EI, which enhanced stock price growth. Once the monetary effect is removed, the adjusted index performed similarly during both periods.

Stock market behavior: effect of real economic conditions

Figure 4.2 shows the same data for the 1929-1965 cycle as was shown in Figure 4.1 for the 1965-1999 cycle. Once again we see the enormous difference in the index performance during the secular bear market from 1929 to 1949 (the index actually was *down* over a twenty year period!) as compared to the secular bull market from 1949 to 1965. In sharp contrast with the subsequent cycle, we note that the adjusted indexes also show very different performances, just like the unadjusted indexes. Clearly, we cannot blame the monetary environment for the difference in performance between the secular bull and bear markets during this cycle.

Figure 4.2 Stock market performance during the 1929-1965 stock cycle

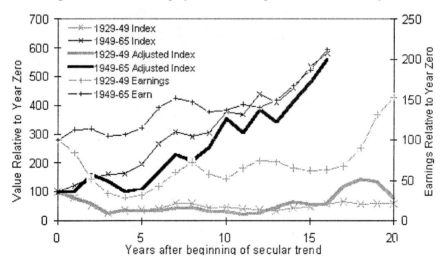

Examination of the earnings profiles shows the culprit. Whereas earnings more than doubled during the secular bull market, earnings fell during the secular bear market and remained lower than their initial value for 18 years. Only towards the very end of the secular bear market

did earnings rise above their initial level, and at that time the monetary environment was unfavorable. Note that the rise in earnings in the late 1940's did give a corresponding increase in the adjusted index. Only in 1949, with a rising earnings trend and improving monetary environment were stocks finally ready to rise, and so the subsequent secular bull market was launched. In this example we see that the cause of the differing performance during the secular bear market (1929-1949) and secular bull market (1949-1965) was *real*, American companies simply did much better in growing earnings during the latter period than the former. Since the former period included the Great Depression this is not really all that surprising.

Figure 4.3 Stock market performance during the 1910-1929 stock cycle

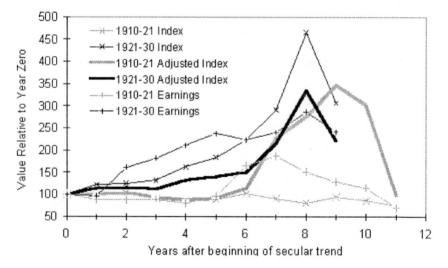

Market performance in earlier cycles

Turning the clock still further back, we look at the next earlier cycle (1910 to 1929). The year 1910 is used as the divider between secular trends rather than 1906 to make the trends more similar in length, easing comparison. The index was higher in *real* terms in 1906 than in 1910, but in nominal terms they were about the same. Nominal earnings were higher in 1910 than in 1906.

Figure 4.3 shows the same set of data as the previous two figures. Again we see a four-fold rise in the index during the secular bull market compared to a decline during the secular bear market. In contrast, the monetary-adjusted indices show similar performances for the two periods, making this cycle most similar to 1966-99. By analogy with the latter cycle, we would expect that the difference in stock performance during the bull and bear portions of this cycle reflected a difference in inflation/interest rates, and not earnings. And we would be right. Inflation ran at double-digit rates in the teens versus mild deflation during the twenties. Excellent earnings growth occurred during the period around World War I and in the 1920's.

A "monetary cycle" in 1965-1999 was preceded by a "real cycle" in 1929-1965, which in turn was preceded by yet another monetary cycle. This suggests a pattern of alternating real and monetary cycles. If this is true, we should expect that the cycle before 1910 would be a real cycle. We would expect the different performance during the bull and bear portions of the cycle to reflect earnings and not the monetary environment (like 1929-1949). We should expect the adjusted indexes to show behavior similar to that of the unadjusted index, and that both should track earnings. Figure 4.4 shows exactly this. During the 1881-1896 secular bear market, both the adjusted and unadjusted indices fell right along with earnings. During the 1896-1910 secular bull market both indices rose right along with earnings.

Figure 4.4. Stock market performance during the 1881-1910 stock cycle

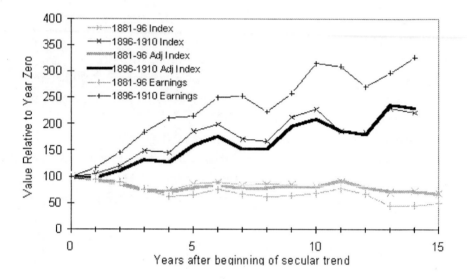

So far, we have identified a pattern of alternating real and monetary stock cycles. In the real cycles, real business performance (as measured by earnings growth) is simply better during the bull periods than it is during the bears. In the monetary cycles, business performance may be similar during both periods, but the impact of the monetary environment on how this performance is valued by the market is different. Applying this idea again we should expect that the 1853-1881 stock cycle should be of the monetary type. That is, it should be like the 1910-1929 and 1966-1999 cycles. Specifically it should have an inflationary (rising EI) secular bear market followed by a disinflationary (falling EI) secular bull market.

Figure 4.5 shows selected information for the Civil War (1853-1881) stock cycle. As we expected, there indeed was an inflationary period, indicated by a rising EI from 1853 to 1864, followed by a disinflationary period, indicated by a falling EI from 1864 to 1881. The index performance for the two periods is also shown. Here we see something different. Index performance was not that different for both periods, unlike what we saw for the other monetary-type cycles. In fact the ordinary index seems to perform much like we would expect the adjusted index to perform.

Earnings are not available before 1871, so nominal GDP (not adjusted for inflation) is plotted as a proxy for earnings. The GDP grew strongly during the Civil War, suggesting that earnings grew as well, just as they grew strongly during WW I (Figure 4.3). The stock index grew along with earnings, unlike what happened during WW I. It would seem that the stock market had not yet "learned" to take inflation into account in valuing earnings at the time of the Civil War, but had so learned by the time of WW I and afterward.

The unadjusted index during the Civil War cycle behaves like the adjusted index does for the subsequent cycles and responds to earnings only, ignoring the inflation rate. Thus, there is no need to plot the adjusted index for this and earlier cycles. So stocks should simply respond to earnings (or GDP) for this and all earlier cycles. As a result of this ignoring of inflation, the 1861-1864 period, although clearly inflationary, falls into the 1861-1881 secular bull market. The inflation-adjusted index rose over 1861-1864 despite the high inflation. It would appear that strong, probably war-enhanced, earnings growth occurred at this time, driving stocks explosively upward.

Figure 4.5 Stock market performance during the 1853-1881 stock cycle

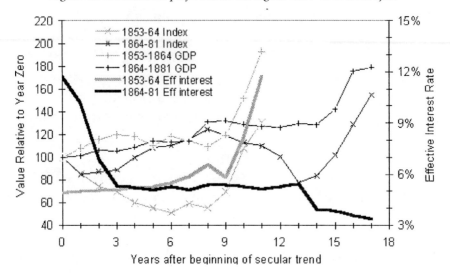

The 1853-1861 period showed fairly flat GDP growth, plus there was the short depression and stock market crash following the Panic of 1857. As a result 1853-1861 was a bear market period. I call it a secular bear market since it comes between the 1843-1853 and the 1861-1881 secular bull markets, but its duration was short enough that it could be considered as a single ordinary bear market. Based on our understanding of secular trends, had the market during the Civil War cycle paid attention to inflation like the modern market does, the secular bear market would have run from 1853 to 1864 and the secular bull market from 1864 to 1881. There would have been a more balanced cycle with an 11-year bear (39%) and a 17-year bull (61%) portion in a 28-year cycle. Instead, there was a lopsided 8-year bear (29%) and 20 year bull period (71%).

The next cycle we consider is the Antebellum cycle (1835-1853). It should be of the real type like 1929-1965 and 1881-1910. We should expect the stock index to follow a rising GDP trend during the secular bull market portion of the cycle (1842-1853) and to follow a falling GDP trend during the secular bear market portion (1835-1842). Figure 4.6 shows exactly that. As a real cycle it simply mirrored the economic trend.

The last cycle we will consider is the Good Feelings cycle (1802-1835). We should expect this cycle to be yet another monetary-type cycle. As a monetary cycle we should expect the difference between the bull and bear portions to be due to the monetary environment, not the earnings or economic growth. That is, we expect nominal GDP growth to be similar during both the secular bull and bear portions of the cycle. Since the early market did not respond to inflation we should expect the regular stock index to behave like the adjusted index does in the later monetary cycles. That is, we should see similar trends in the nominal index during both periods.

Figure 4.6 Stock market performance during the 1835-1853 stock cycle

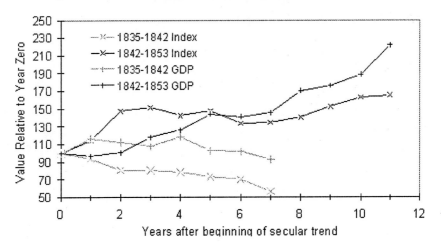

Figure 4.7 shows that the regular index was pretty flat during both the secular bull and bear markets during this cycle. GDP rose by a similar amount during both phases. This is exactly what we would expect for a pre-Civil War monetary cycle. Since the performance of the index was so lackluster during both the Good Feelings bull and bear secular trends, one might wonder why the distinction is even made. The answer is shown in the inflation-adjusted index values, which appear as the bold lines in Figure 4.7. Here we see the large difference in stock performance that characterizes the secular bull and bear markets. It is clear that most of the difference in the real performance comes from changes in the value of the dollar caused by the inflation during 1802-1815 and the deflation during 1815-1835. There is comparatively little effect of changes in the dollar-value of the index. In this earliest monetary cycle the cause of the secular trends is still the monetary cycle, but the trends can only be detected by considering the inflation-adjusted index.

Monetary cycles are more intense today; one reason for today's bull market strength

Since the Civil War cycle there have been two effects of inflation. First inflation reduces the value the market places on earnings, resulting in a flat trend, rather than a rising trend in the index. Secondly, the effect of the cheapening dollar makes the real value of the index fall even further. As a result P/R falls to extremely low levels during inflationary bear markets. Examination of Figure 3.1 shows how the inflationary 1910's and 1970's secular bear markets caused a "crash" in the constant-dollar index. This crash was masked by what appears to be a flat profile in terms of the dollar value of the index (see Figure 3.3).

Once the inflationary period ends, the market now starts to adjust its valuation of earnings upward. First the "old earnings" that were obtained during the inflationary period are valued higher, causing a rise in stock prices without a need for any "new" earnings growth. But earnings growth occurs during the bull market portion of the cycle also. These earnings are also valued at the higher levels typical of a disinflationary period. The result is a double positive effect on the index during the secular bull market portion of monetary cycles. It is no surprise that the post-Civil War monetary cycles have given the most intense stock booms in US history. A significant part of the excellent performance in the monetary cycle secular bull market is simply the market playing catch-up for the enormous losses inflicted (in real terms) by the previous secular bear market.

Figure 4.7 Stock market performance during the 1802-1835 stock cycle

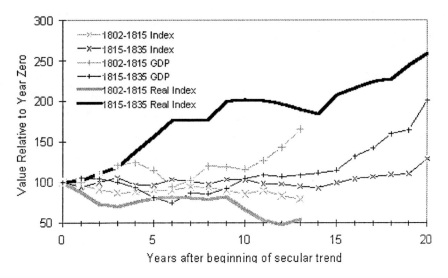

P/R neatly captures this phenomenon as we saw in the discussion concerning Figure 3.3. When the inflationary period begins, the dollar value of R rises. The dollar value of the index does not rise for the reasons described earlier. Hence P/R falls, showing stocks becoming more and more undervalued relative to their future. Although the index is undervalued, it won't rise until after the inflationary period ends. Then it comes roaring upwards like a submerged beach ball suddenly released. This response was shown in 1982-1987, which mostly reflected the market revaluing old earnings that had been created in the 1970's but given a low value because of the unfavorable monetary environment. By 1987 this process was complete (and perhaps a bit overdone as evidenced by the high P/E and crash that year). The new earnings for the bull portion of the cycle had not yet come, as shown by the still low value of P/R. The bull had a long way to run.

In contrast, by 1929 the market had already responded to both the improved monetary environment and the new earnings achieved during the 1920's. This was shown by the high value of P/R, which indicated that the market had pretty much priced in all the potential growth available from the level of business resources at that time. The bull portion of the stock cycle was complete and it was time for a new cycle to begin. The situation today is similar to 1929. The effect of both the monetary conditions and a very optimistic assessment of the earnings growth still to come are priced into the index. This is shown by the extraordinarily high level of P/R. We should expect the current monetary cycle to be followed by a real cycle. It should start with a secular bear market in which lower earnings growth will be the problem, not inflation.

A quantitative description for the stock market index

So far we have described qualitatively how monetary and real economic factors impact stock prices in such a way as to produce stock cycles. We will now try to develop these ideas in a more quantitative fashion. Specifically, we want to see how accurately these ideas can explain today's market and if not, to find what additional factors must be added to explain things today. We will start with a simple model that says that the index value or price (P) is directly related to earnings (E) and inversely related to effective interest rate (i)

4.2 $P \propto E / i$

Equation 4.2 implies that stocks should be valued like a bond. The price paid for a given amount of E will depend on the price that the market is currently paying for income from fixed-income investments like bonds. The ratio of bond income to price is the interest rate, and that is why i appears in the denominator.

Unlike a bond, a stock's earnings are anything but fixed. In the past, stocks tended to be valued based on their dividend payments rather than earnings. Dividends tend to be more constant over time than earnings, but even dividends can be lowered if the company falls on hard times. And in the event of bankruptcy, it is the bondholders who get what assets remain; stockholders are wiped out. As a result, stock investors have traditionally required an extra return over that available from fixed-income investments (bonds) as compensation for the fact that income from a stock is not fixed (it can go down). Stock analysts call this extra return the *risk premium* (rp). A risk premium modifies equation 4.2 as follows:

4.3 $P = E / (i + rp) \Rightarrow E/P = i + rp$

Equation 4.3 merely says that the index price is inversely proportional to the adjusted interest rate plus a risk premium rather than just the interest rate (as would be the case for a bond). Equation 4.3 can be rewritten in terms of the earnings yield (E/P), which can be thought of as sort of an "implicit income" rate for the stock. We expect this yield to depend on the fixed-income yield plus some extra return (rp) to reflect the fact that E is not fixed. Figure 4.8 shows a plot of the earnings yield, effective interest rate and risk premium for the years 1871 to 1999. From 1871-1960, the earnings yield has tended to follow i in a manner consistent with a risk premium of 3-5% (average 3.7%). After 1960, the risk premium started a long-term decline. The negative risk premium of the last 10-15 years, combined with falling interest rates over the past decade have produced the remarkably low earnings yield of today, about 3% lower than the prevailing long-term interest rate.

The valuation idea expressed in equation 4.3 implies that the index should be valued on its earnings power, that is, its ability to produce current income. This income can be paid out to the stockholder in the form of dividends or reinvested back into the businesses that comprise the index. Dividend income provides a direct return. Reinvestment of retained earnings increases R, which will eventually show up as higher real prices, producing real capital gains for the stockholder. Taking both modes of return together, the total real return on stocks (over the long run) should be equal to the earnings yield. Since the P/E on the stock index is the reciprocal of the earnings yield, the average P/E should equal the reciprocal of the long-term return. As we noted in chapter 2, this long-term return is about 6.8%, the reciprocal of which is 14.7. Historically, P/E has averaged about 14.3 over the long run, which is consistent with this analysis.

Figure 4.8. Earnings yield and effective interest rates over time

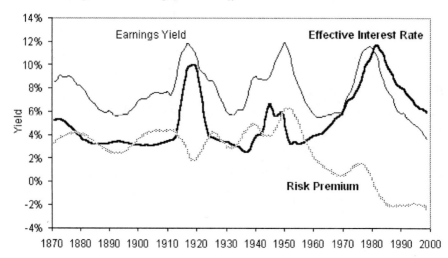

Today's P/E on the S&P500 is over 30, indicating that stocks are more than twice the price consistent with their long term return. If P/E permanently stays at this level, the long-term return in the future will fall from 6.8% to about 3% (the reciprocal of a P/E of 30+). To maintain high rates of return into the distant future, the index P/E has to come down. A reduction in P/E necessarily requires that returns will be very poor while this is happening. The prediction using P/R in the first chapter says this return-preserving reduction in P/E will occur soon.

But suppose it doesn't? When the risk premium first started to drop in the late 1950's stock experts warned that the stock market was becoming dangerously overvalued.[10] Their warnings were based on the sort of analysis just outlined and was (and is) perfectly sound. But the market did not crash, instead the risk premium continued to fall. A fundamental shift in the way investors viewed stocks had apparently occurred. This drop in risk premium coupled with the recent trend towards lower interest rates have today given rise to P/E's far higher than 14, and far higher than any before seen. Could another shift be occurring? Some market commentators argue that a new paradigm of stock valuation has occurred and that stocks will permanently have higher valuations[11] (and lower returns). They point to the shift in valuation paradigm in 1960 as an example that such things can occur.

We need to consider this argument seriously. If the market of the future is going to consistently award sky-high P/E's to minuscule earnings, extremely high levels of P/R will become the norm. If this happens, the market will continue to rise for some time, after which returns will settle down to perhaps half their historic average. The prediction of poor returns in the intermediate term made in chapter two would keep us out of the market for the last few good years it will ever have.

On the other hand, suppose the high P/E of today is simply the continuation of the same paradigm shift made around 1960, simply applied to the situation of today. That is, the same valuation concepts that explain the markets levels in the 1960's 1970's and 1980's also explain the valuations of the late 1990's. If we can show that this is the case, then today's high P/E does *not* mean that there is a new view of stocks and all comparison to history is invalid. Specifically, since the new post-1960 valuation paradigm did not prevent a secular bear market from arriving in 1966, there is no historical basis for indicating we won't have another one in the near future. In the next section we describe a model for the post-1960 market that explains the high valuation of today in terms of decades-old concepts acting on the special economic conditions of today. In other words, there is no new paradigm and today's high P/Es are nothing new.

A more sophisticated model for the post-1960 market

The usual explanation for the high P/E today is that models like equation 4.3 do not account for the fact that earnings grow over time. The idea of a positive risk premium for stocks came from the fact that the income from stocks can fall, while income from bonds is fixed. But the income from stocks can also rise, in which case a negative earnings premium would be in order. Historically, the income derived from stocks rises over the long run. The long term rising trend in the stock market depicted in Figures 2.1 and 3.1 illustrates this fact. The higher value for stocks justified by their future growth is shown mathematically through the use of a discount earnings model, which estimates the value of a growing earnings stream.

The idea of discounting future performance was introduced in chapter three. The impact of "discount-thinking" can be illustrated with a few examples. First we look at the case of no discounting and then the effect of discounting over longer and longer periods of time. Long term interest rates have averaged about 5.9% in 1999 and the earnings yield on the S&P500 about 3.1% (P/E of 32). Application of equation 4.3 with the pre-1960 average risk premium of 3.7% would give a projected earnings yield of 9.6% (P/E of 10.4) for today. Today's index is priced three times higher than it would be if the pre-1960 paradigm was still in effect. It would appear that the effect of discounting can be pretty significant.

Over the 1990's earnings grew at a 10.7% rate. Let us assume that earnings continue to grow at this rate for two more years, at which point growth is halted by a recession. At that point, valuation using equation 4.3 with the historical risk premium of 3.7% would be a sensible proposition. With these assumptions, what is the present value of the index? The value indicated by a discounted earnings calculation would be about 15 times earnings. Now assume that earnings grow for another four years instead of two. In this case the discounted earnings calculation gives a P/E of about 20 for the index today. To obtain the recent P/E of 32, we need to discount eight years of 10.7% earnings growth. The steady drop in risk premium over the last forty years implies an increasing discount period has been employed for valuation. That is, more and more future has been incorporated into the market P/E. Figure 4.9 shows a reason why the market has been doing this.

Figure 4.9. Length of economic expansions since 1854.

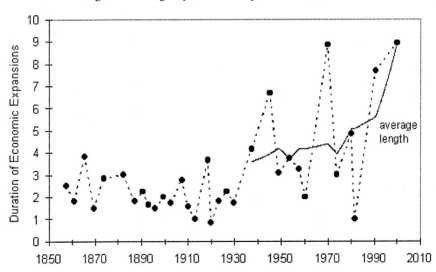

It is apparent from Figure 4.9 that the length of economic expansions has increased over the last six or seven decades, and especially over the last couple of decades. With a longer expansion today, it is not surprising that the market discounts over a longer period of time than it did in the past. A model was constructed that uses this idea of an increasing discount period equal to the average expansion length as shown in Figure 4.9. The details of its construction are given in Appendix A. Here we will simply present some results obtained with it. Figure 4.10 shows the model results, the actual index value and the deviation between them for the post 1960 period.

The fit between the model and the index is quite good. On average, the deviation has been about 12%. Three periods of extreme positive deviation have occurred. In each case the discrepancy between the index and model closed shortly afterward. One of these was in 1987, which was closed by the index falling down to the model level in the October crash. In this case it was clear that the market was short-term overvalued. In 1970 and the early 1990's, large positive deviations also occurred. Both of these periods were during a recession. It was rational for investors to accord a premium value to the index (relative to the model) since it was likely that when the recession ended, stock fundamentals would rebound and the model with them. This is exactly what happened, the positive deviation was closed by a rise in the model rather than a fall in the index.

Another thing we note is the flat region in the model between 1965 and 1979. Here we see the secular bear market reflected in the economic fundamentals. The index was significantly below the model only once, in the 1979-1980 period. This negative deviation was rational since the model fell back to the index value in the 1982 recession. These four examples of deviations show us that the market gets it right most of the time.

Figure 4.10 Application of market model to the stock market after 1960

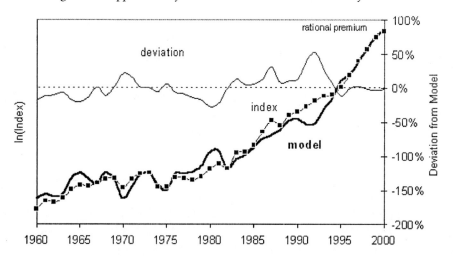

What can we learn from this model about today's market?

Figure 4.10 shows that the index values of today agree very well with the model. Not only is the index not overvalued (relative to the fundamentals as described by the model), but as long as the earnings growth trend remains intact, the index will keep rising. For example, if we assume that the earnings growth of the past five years persists indefinitely into the future, without interruption by any recession, the model reaches a value of 5,000 by 2007 (corresponding to a Dow of 35,000) and 15,000 by 2016 (corresponding to a Dow of 100,000). Here we see how the model (with rather optimistic economic projections) is consistent with the bullish projections made by a number of popular books of Dow 35,000[12] by 2007, 40,000[13] by 2016 or 100,000[14] by 2020.

But a 17-26 year economic expansion would have to occur for these wondrous results to come to pass, which seems unlikely. What would happen if the current expansion ended right now? The Federal Reserve has been hiking interest rates recently, in an attempt to slow down a red-hot economy. Suppose instead of a slowdown, a recession happens instead. Before addressing this scenario, I must stress that this model is descriptive rather than predictive. We can describe possible consequences given certain economic inputs, but we cannot tell exactly how the market will respond to a given set of economic inputs. Nor can we predict future economic inputs. With this caveat firmly in mind, let us explore the consequences of a recession that begins this year (2000).

Impact of a Recession

To examine the impact of a recession, we need an example of a recession. Let us use a repeat of the 1990 recession that begins right now (Jan 2000) as our hypothetical recession. The S&P500 earnings peaked in June 1989, marking the end of the 1980's earnings expansion. We will use the month-to-month percentage changes in earnings, effective interest rates and index value that followed June 1989 to predict the future course of these variables. We will apply this series of changes to the current market beginning in January 2000. Doing so we obtain an earnings trough on the S&P500 index in August 2002, down 36% from the January 2000 peak. This date marks the recession trough in terms of earnings. Interest rates would be at about 5.5%, down about 1% from the January 2000 level. The market index would be at about 1760, up from 1475 in January 2000, giving a P/E of about 60. Is this a reasonable scenario?

To answer this question we need to consider the market dynamics at the 1992 earnings low resulting from the 1990 recession. At the earnings trough in 1992, S&P500 index earnings stood at $16. Given the average earnings of $16.3 in the 1980's and the long term earnings growth rate of 6.3% per year, one could have projected an average value for S&P500 earnings of $30 for the decade of the 1990's (in actual fact this average was $29.3 so this would have been an excellent projection). If we enter 30 for earnings into the model in 1992 we obtain a value of 450, which is 16% higher than the index value of 388 at that time. That is, valuing the very likely future earnings of $30 under the same conditions as the present (1992) gave a value higher than where the index stood in 1992. So it was rational for the market to wait and see how things turned out. By 1995, the index earnings reached the projected earnings of $30 and the index reached 455, almost exactly what we predicted from the model in 1992. Thus the overvaluation relative to the model in 1992 had vanished *without the index going down*. This is why I referred to the premium price in the early 1990's as a rational premium.

Now let us look at the hypothetical situation in 2002. Using the same arguments as above we could surmise that in the 2000's the average earnings would be $55. If we enter 55 for the earnings in the model for 2002, we would obtain a value of about 1360, which is 23% *less* than the 1760 projected value on the index. With an estimated future value of 1360, it would be irrational for the market to be at 1760 during a recession bottom in 2002. The index in 2002 should be less than the projected future value of 1360, just as the value of the index in 1992 (388) was less than the projected future value of 450.

Suppose that the index is at 1140 at the earnings bottom in 2002. Once again we enter 55 into the model to predict the index level after recovery and we obtain two answers: 650 and 1360. The lower value corresponds to the case where the market projects the recession to be lengthy and that the subsequent expansion will be shorter than the last one. The higher value corresponds to the case where the market projects the recession to be brief and the subsequent expansion to be long. A value of 1140 for an index with a projected range of future values of 650-1360 seems a little high. A lower value for the index seems more reasonable. But the lower the index goes, the more likely the market will adopt a bearish view of the future (650) and the less likely it will have a bullish view (1360).

This example illustrates what the financier George Soros refers to as the principle of reflexivity.[15] As long as the market is going up, the more rosy projections have greater credence. These rosy projections justify the current prices and even higher ones in the future. But, once the market starts going down in a convincing fashion, more dire projections gain credence and justify lower prices. The model captures this reflexivity by shifting between optimistic and pessimistic views of the future, depending on recent market performance.

Development of a secular bear market

Recall the discussion about the proposed mechanism by which P/R works. Maximum values of P/R are caused by maximum values in ROR. Once the limiting value of ROR is reached, further growth in earnings will be slowed. At the end of the current expansion ROR will likely be at its peak value for the cycle. Following the recession it is unlikely that earnings will continue to rise during the next expansion at the same rate as over the last decade. This means we will have either weak expansions (slower growth) or strong expansions of short duration with more frequent recessions. Shorter expansions will reduce the discount time and slower growth will reduce earnings. Either way, the valuations given by the model would drop, resulting in a succession of failed bull markets, in short, a secular bear market.

Summary

In this chapter we saw how long-term shifts in either the monetary or the business (earnings) environment give rise to the secular bull and bear markets that make up the stock cycles. We constructed a model to represent these ideas in a more quantitative fashion. We saw how the high current P/E on the S&P500 index reflects the application of discount thinking to the enormously long economic expansion we have enjoyed. No new concepts were needed. We could see that a serious bear market will probably develop if a recession occurs. And if that recession were followed by an expansion of more ordinary length, or with slower earnings growth, the model suggests that a secular bear market would be the result. This is the same prediction made in previous chapters. The difference here is we have identified the short-term factors that need to be present for it to actually happen. For example, we will need a recession (or fear of one) to end this current bull market. And earnings growth will have to slow afterward, likely because of shorter expansions.

We have learned that the operation of the stock cycle is dependent on the economy. Stock cycles reflect economic cycles. In the next chapter we will learn that the alternating monetary and real cycles are a manifestation of an economic cycle called the Kondratiev cycle.

Chapter Five

The Kondratiev Cycle

We have seen how stocks have displayed alternating periods of good and bad performance that together constitute a stock cycle. Stock cycles alternate between monetary cycles and real cycles. In the former, the differential in performance between secular bull and bear markets reflects the monetary environment, while in the latter, performance difference is based on the business conditions. We can combine two stock cycles into one longer cycle containing one monetary cycle and one real cycle. These cycles, which average 56 years in length, would serve as the shortest repeating unit in a system of repetitive stock market cycles. Since the stock market cycles are simply reflections of the underlying economy, we should expect an economic cycle to exist with an average length of about 56 years. Such a *long cycle* had been postulated by the Russian economist Nikolai Kondratiev, who was the first to describe it in detail.[16]

The Kondratiev cycle theory holds that capitalistic economies grow in a cyclic fashion with an average periodicity of about 50 years. This cycle is shown most clearly by the behavior of prices, inflation and interest rates, which rise and fall over time. The maximum in prices or inflation occurs at the Kondratiev peak (K-peak). The minimum occurs at the Kondratiev trough (K-trough). The period of rising prices leading up to the K-peak is called the upwave and the period of falling prices is the downwave.

The price cycles of different countries tend to move in phase. Kondratiev looked at prices and interest rates in Great Britain, France, the U.S. and Germany. Numerous researchers have studied long cycles since the time of Kondratiev. Joshua Goldstein[17] summarizes the work of thirty-three scholars in his excellent book on long cycles. He presents composite estimates for K-peaks and K-troughs that he calls his base dating scheme. Although I could simply present Goldstein's dates, it is useful to look at the actual data to get a feel for the nature of these cycles. We will focus on cycles in the U.S. since 1800 because we are primarily concerned with the U.S. stock market behavior since 1800. We will also examine cycles in Great Britain from before 1800 to provide additional examples of such cycles.

The strategy taken will be to examine the history of prices and more recently, inflation rates to determine long term maximum and minimum values, which are then potential K-peaks and K-troughs. I will then present a number of arguments to assess which of these peaks and troughs truly are Kondratiev points.

The Kondratiev Price Cycle for the U.S.

Figure 5.1 shows U.S. price/inflation data. For the period 1720 to 1940 the line in the figure presents the level of producer prices. Producer prices were selected because data exists for them further back than it does for consumer prices. Also in an agricultural/industrial economy, producer prices are more relevant. Since 1940 the U.S. economy has experienced near-continuous inflation with almost no price deflation. A plot of prices would show an almost uninterrupted rise. Thus, for the years after 1940 the annual rate of inflation in consumer prices is plotted. The inflation rate was smoothed by a three year moving average with double weight on the center year. Consumer price inflation was selected because during the 1930's the economy became over 50% service-based, for which consumer prices are more relevant. The price and inflation plots were spliced together and the latter scaled to give a similar degree of fluctuation throughout the entire period. Interpretation of the figure is simple. Peaks represent maximum values in prices (before 1940) or inflation rate (after 1940). Similarly, valleys represent minimum values in prices or inflation. Prior to 1940 the rising portions of the graph represent inflation and the falling portions deflation. After 1940, the rising portions represent accelerating prices (rising inflation) whereas the falling sections represent decelerating prices (disinflation).

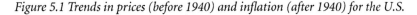

Figure 5.1 Trends in prices (before 1940) and inflation (after 1940) for the U.S.

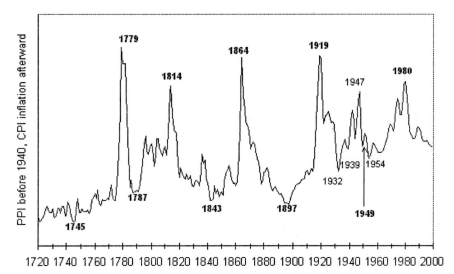

Six price peaks are labeled in the figure, five of them (in bold) marking Kondratiev peaks. For each of the K-peaks one can see rising prices before the peak and falling ones afterward during periods of peace (no economic stimulus by government). This is what makes them K-peaks.

A bout of high inflation caused by massive fiscal stimulus (due to war spending for example), sandwiched between two periods of falling prices/inflation would not be a K-peak. An upwave should contain periods of rising prices in the absence of massive Government spending. Therefore, the 1947 inflation peak associated with World War II inflation is not considered a Kondratiev peak. Prices in the 1920's and early 1930's were falling. Inflation in the 1950's and 1960's was rising. Somewhere between 1932 and 1954 there has to be a K-trough. If 1947 were to be a K-peak then there would have to be two K-troughs between 1932 and 1954. This would give an entire Kondratiev cycle only 22 years long at most.

The economist Don Roper[18] advances the hypothesis that what makes the longwave isn't the inflationary episode per se, but rather the response of the monetary system after the inflation. During wartime, monetary restraint is relaxed in order to meet the national emergency. Afterward, high real interest rates drive up the value of money to restore pre-war levels of monetary rectitude. It is these high real interest rates that cause the downwave to begin, a process that typically takes decades to be completed. Consider the five large price peaks since 1800 in Figure 5.1. The average real interest rate for the eight years after these peaks was 10.3% after 1814, 6.6% after 1864, 4.3% after 1919, 0.4% after 1947 and 5.8% after 1980. All these rates (except one) are higher than the average value of 3.1% over the entire period since 1800. The exception was following 1947, when rates were much *lower* than the long-term average. In the first four cases, there was a significant amount of monetary tightening after the inflationary episode. In the last case there was not. Clearly, 1947 is not a Kondratiev peak according to Roper's definition.

Figure 5.2. Inflation and interest rates in the 1947-1960 period

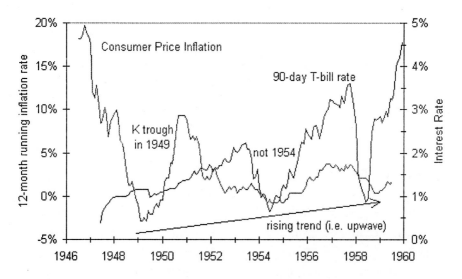

Next we consider the seven troughs in Figure 5.1. The 1745, 1787, 1843 and 1897 troughs in the figure are close to the U.S. K-trough dates assigned by other scholars.[17] The next trough is more problematic. It would seem that 1932 is the obvious candidate. It was a bona fide price trough and inflation was nearly -10%. There were also troughs in 1939, 1949 and 1954, as shown in Figure 5.1. Goldstein's base scheme gives 1940.[17] Economist Brian Berry[19], a modern researcher of the longwave, favors 1954, which appears natural enough in the smoothed trends shown in Figure 5.1. Figure 5.2 shows running 12-month inflation and interest rates for the period 1947-1959. Inflation and interest rates bottomed in the late 1940's and started to rise afterward, supporting the choice of 1949 as a trough.

The price structure of the 1932-1954 period is complicated by the massive governmental stimulus of the economy produced by the New

Deal and World War II, which produced inflation during what would ordinarily be the downwave. If we look at those (few) years when the government ran small deficits or even a surplus, we can get an idea of what the unstimulated economy was doing. The U.S. government ran the smallest deficit of the New Deal era in 1938 at 1.3% of revenue. Prices fell 2% in that year and the economy fell into recession, suggesting that the downwave was still in operation and the 1934-37 inflation had been caused by fiscal stimulation from New Deal spending. This observation rules out 1932 as a K-trough and makes 1939 the earliest candidate for K-trough.

The government ran a surplus from 1947 to 1949, during which time inflation collapsed and deflation appeared (see Figure 5.2). As discussed above, this collapse in inflation occurred without the need for high real interest rates to reverse inflationary tendencies. Simply the removal of stimulus did the job. This suggests that a deflationary tendency was still in operation in these years. In contrast, when the government ran a basically balanced budget from 1954-58, inflation and interest rates rose, implying we had entered an upwave. Therefore, the K-trough was in either 1949 or 1954. To break the deadlock we turn to the stock cycles. We note that the secular bull market portion of the real stock cycle began in 1843, 1896 and 1949. The first two dates are within one year of the 1843 and 1897 K-troughs. This correspondence between an important stock cycle marker and an important Kondratiev cycle marker makes it logical to pick 1949 as the K-trough.

The five U.S. troughs have an average spacing of 51 years. The five peaks have an average spacing of 50 years. All together, the average cycle length for the U.S. is 51 years.

Figure 5.3 British prices from 1475 to 1900 showing K-peaks and troughs

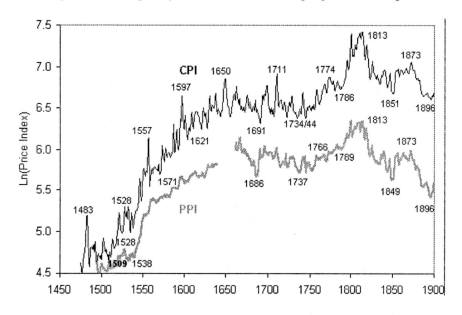

The Kondratiev Price Cycle for Great Britain

Figure 5.3 shows a consumer price index (CPI) and a producer price index (PPI) for the British economy over the period 1475-1900. The Kondratiev peaks and troughs are labeled. The eighteenth century peaks and troughs were particularly difficult to assess. Producer prices peaked in 1696, during the War of the League of Augsburg (1689-97). Consumer Prices showed a peak in 1699 following this war, but a still higher peak occurred in 1711, during the War of the Spanish Succession (1702-13).

Interest rates reached their highest level of the century in 1711, so this date was selected as the K-peak. Both consumer and producer prices troughed in the 1734-44 period. Aside from the low interest rate associated with the South Sea fiasco in 1720 (see chapter 7), interest rates reached their lowest levels of the century in 1737. Averaging the CPI, PPI and the interest rate low together gives 1738 as the date for the K-trough. Consumer prices put in a small peak in 1774 and a small trough in 1786. Producer prices showed no significant peaks or troughs around this time. Interest rates peaked in 1762, associated with the Seven Years War (1756-63) and again in 1782, associated with the American Revolution (1776-1783).

To select the next K-peak and K-trough, inflation rates over successive fifteen year periods were calculated and examined for the 1730-1800 period. Consumer price inflation showed a minimum in 1739, a maximum in 1774 and a minimum in 1787. Producer price inflation showed a minimum in 1740, a maximum in 1766 and a minimum in 1792. Interest rates showed a trough in 1737, peaks in 1762 and 1782 and a trough in 1791. The late 1730's troughs in CPI, PPI and interest rates correspond nicely with the assignment of 1738 as K-trough. The troughs in CPI, PPI and interest rates around 1790, also correspond nicely with a date of 1789 for the subsequent K-trough. The 1762 interest rate peak was averaged with the two inflation rate peaks in give 1767 as an estimate for the K-peak. Alternately, the 1782 interest rate peak could be averaged with the inflation peaks to give 1774. The first of these is closer to the three underlying peaks than the second, and so it was chosen as an estimate for the K-peak.

Table 5.1. Kondratiev Peaks and Troughs from 1460

British Economy		U.S. Economy		Goldstein's Base Dating Scheme	
Trough	Peak	Trough	Peak	Trough	Peak
--	1483	--	--	1460[*]	1483[*]
1509	1528	--	--	1509	1529
1538	1557	--	--	1539	1559
1571	1597	--	--	1575	1595
1621	1650	--	--	1621	1650
1689	1711	--	--	1689	1720
1738	1767	1745	1779	1747	1762
1789	1813	1787	1814	1790	1814
1849	1873	1843	1864	1848	1872
1896	1920	1897	1919	1893	1917
1949	1977	1949	1980	1940	1980

*Goldstein's study starts in 1495, these values are from Braudel[27]

The K-troughs and peaks for both the British and U.S. economies are presented in Table 5.1. Also shown is the base dating scheme given by Goldstein.[18] The correspondence is very good between the dates given here and those given by Goldstein, showing the uniformity of the cycle across different national economies. There have been ten trough-to-trough British cycles since 1460 and ten peak-peak cycles since 1483. The cycle lengths have ranged from 29 to 68 years with an average length of 49 years. If we focus on the three cycles since 1787, we obtain an average length of 54 years for the British cycles and 55 years for the American cycles, which agrees well with the 56 year double stock cycle. Figures 5.1 and 5.3 with Table 5.1 shows the principal evidence for the existence of a 50 year cycle in prices that goes back centuries.

Relation of the Kondratiev Cycle to Economic Cycles and the Stock Cycle

Most economists acknowledge that long cycles in prices have occurred, at least since the Industrial Revolution. The evidence in Figure 5.1 is pretty convincing. Where heated disagreements spring up is when one extends the idea of Kondratiev periodicity to real economic variables such as growth in GDP or real wages. Comparisons between the Kondratiev cycle and stock markets don't seem to be made, at least I haven't seen any. In this section we look at some evidence for cycles in real GDP and then go on to draw comparisons between nominal GDP, prices and stock index levels that we will use for assigning our position within the Kondratiev cycle.

Figure 5.4 shows a plot of real GDP per capita divided by the 100-year trend in GDP per capita. The trend value is simply the log-regression line of GDP per capita with time over a hundred-year period centered on the year of interest. For example, the trend value for 1850 is the log-regression fit of the data between 1800 and 1900. For the years before 1839, the period 1789-1889 was used to determine the trend. For the years after 1949 the 1899-1999 period was employed. The ratios between GDP and trend GDP were smoothed using a five-year moving average centered on each year. The labels represent the peak and trough years determined from this smoothed trend.

Figure 5.4 Real GDP per capita relative to its 100-year trend for the period 1789-1999

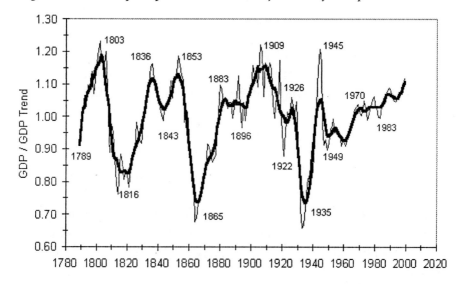

The idea behind Figure 5.4 is that the economy grows at a fairly steady pace over the long run (see Figure 3.2). By fitting a trend line to 100 years of data, we should get a pretty good approximation of where the GDP "should" be in the absence of cyclic deviations from the trend. Plotting the ratio of GDP to the trend value in effect plots the cyclical deviations shown by GDP over time. One of these deviations is the familiar 5-10 year business cycle with its alternating expansions and recessions. Another type of cyclic fluctuation are the slowdowns and speedups that occur sporadically at more frequent intervals (e.g. the Fed dealt with one of these speedups in 1994 by hiking interest rates to produce a slowdown). The five-year moving average effectively removes these short-term perturbations and dampens out the business cycle, leaving longer cycles largely intact.

The figure shows semi-periodic fluctuations of 17 to 33 years (25 average) which define an economic cycle first described by the Russian-American economist Simon Kuznets.[20] The rising portions of the cycle reflect periods when per capita GDP advanced at a faster rate than the long-term trend and can be considered expansionary periods. The falling portions of the cycle can be thought of as recessionary periods. Inspection of Figure 5.4 shows that there were roughly two Kuznets cycles per Kondratiev cycle for the first two Kondratievs. The combination of Kuznets and Kondratiev cycles define four subperiods in the longwave. The investment analyst P. Q. Wall[21] has given seasonal names to these subperiods: Spring and Summer are the expansionary and recessionary phases of the upwave Kuznets cycle. Fall and Winter are the corresponding periods during the downwave. Table 5.2 presents dates for the Kondratiev, Kuznets and stock cycles in the U.S. since 1787.

Table 5.2 The Kondratiev, Kuznets and Stock Cycles

Kondratiev Cycle		Kuznets Cycle		Stock Cycle	
I - upwave	1787-1814	Spring	1789-1803		
		Summer	1803-1816	monetary bear	1802-1815
I - downwave	1814-1843	Fall	1816-1836	monetary bull	1815-1835
		Winter	1836-1843	"real" bear	1835-1843
II - upwave	1843-1864	Spring	1843-1853	"real" bull	1843-1853
		Summer	1853-1865	monetary bear	1853-1861
II -downwave	1864-1897	Fall	1865-1883	monetary bull	1861-1881
		Winter	1883-1896	"real" bear	1881-1896
III - upwave	1897-1919	Spring	1896-1909	"real" bull	1896-1906
		Summer	1909-1922	monetary bear	1906-1921
III -downwave	1919-1949	Fall	1922-1926	monetary bull	1921-1929
		Winter	1926-1935	"real" bear	1929-1949
		"False Spring"	1935-1945		
		more Winter	1945-1949		
IV - upwave	1949-1980	Spring	1949-1970	"real" bull	1949-1966
		Summer	1970-1983	monetary bear	1966-1982
IV-downwave	1980-	Fall	1983-	monetary bull	1982-

Table 5.2 shows that there is a rough correspondence between the Kuznets cycle and the stock cycle except for the period around the Depression and World War II. Basically, the secular bear portion of a monetary stock cycle is "Summer" while the secular bull portion is "Fall". The secular bear portion of a real stock cycle is "Winter", while the bull portion is "Spring". For the first two Kondratievs all three cycles lined up very well. For the third cycle there was one Kuznets and stock cycle during the upwave, but an extra cycle was added by the Depression and World War II. There was an upswing or "false spring" in the Kuznets cycle from 1935 to 1945 during what would ordinarily be winter. After 1945 winter resumed giving a low in 1949 (unsmoothed) or 1960 (smoothed). Following this low is a rising trend to 1970, which represents spring of the fourth Kondratiev.

A combination of monetary factors (prices & interest rates) and real factors (economic performance) cause stock cycles as we saw in chapter four. The Kondratiev cycle deals with cyclic changes in monetary factors and the Kuznets cycle deals with cyclic changes in economic perform-ance. So it is not surprising that the stock cycle should line up well with the Kondratiev and Kuznets cycles.

The Kuznets cycle after 1945 no longer shows strong fluctuations, probably because of government policies designed to dampen economic fluctuations. Unlike GDP, the stock market displays very strong cycles, which continue to line up with the Kondratiev cycle, two per cycle. The extraordinary stock gains in recent years results from investors discount-ing future earnings growth over longer periods of time. This makes the market extraordinarily leveraged to the economy. This leverage allows today's weak Kuznets cycle to produce a strong stock cycle.

The most recent Kuznets summer (1970-1983) showed up as a change in the *duration* of expansions rather than a major slump like previous summers. The average length of economic expansions was shorter during the 1970's than they were either before or since. This coming winter season could also be characterized by short business cycles like in 1883-1896 rather than a lengthy slump like in the Depression. Shortened expansions would gradually shift the market from a future-orientated to a present-orientated valuation scheme, resulting in a contraction in P/E. The result would be a secular bear market as the valuations slowly adjust, even though economic growth might be fairly good. This, of course, is what is predicted to be imminent by P/R.

On the other hand, the absence of a strong Kuznets cycle since 1945 may mean that there will be no Winter. So, although there is no new paradigm of stock valuation there may be a "new era" of the economy brought about by the Internet and modern macroeconomics management which will eliminate, or at least moderate, the impact of business cycles. As we did with the new paradigm argument, we need to see if the "old" model of the Kondratiev cycle can or cannot explain the current economic environment. If the former, then we have to retain the possibility that the cycles are still with us. If not, then there is a whole new range of investment possibilities for us to seriously consider. To explore this idea more closely, we must specify our position within the cycle as precisely as possible in order to draw appropriate parallels with history. To do that we will need to explore the Kondratiev cycle in more detail.

Fine structure of the Kondratiev cycle

Figure 5.5 shows the fine structure of the U.S. price/inflation history since 1800. After the K-peak there is a rapid drop-off in prices (or inflation). After a few years, the decline slows, or even reverses and a small peak may appear. This period is called the plateau. The plateau is followed by a second drop in prices/inflation culminating in a low called the vortex by Berry.[19] After the vortex low there is a second rise in prices/inflation, stronger than the plateau, that peaks at what I call the deflationary (disinflationary) growth peak or DG-peak. Following the DG peak prices (inflation) fall again, reaching a low at the K-trough.

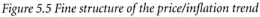

Figure 5.5 Fine structure of the price/inflation trend

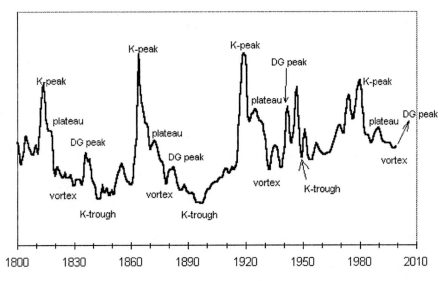

Figure 5.6 shows a plot of annual growth rates in *nominal* per capita GDP for the downwave portion of the four U.S. Kondratiev cycles since 1787. Nominal refers to the data *not* corrected for inflation, so these data are different from those in Figure 5.4, which are corrected for inflation. The data are lined up relative to the K-peak for each cycle and show plateau, vortex and DG-peaks similar in location and shape to the same structures in the price plot. We notice that both the plateau and the vortex from the current downwave line up well with the previous cycles. At present we are entering the region of the DG peak. So the recent rise in inflation and strong economic growth is perfectly normal for this period in the downwave. A strong stock market is also normal.

For example, if we look back at the last three cycles, we find that the four-year period of fastest peacetime economic growth during the Kondratiev cycle has occurred during the expansion leading up to the DG peak: 1830-1833 for the first cycle, 1877-1880 for the second cycle and 1934-37 for the third cycle. Looking at the stock market we see four year annualized real returns of 13% in 1831-35, 30% in 1877-1881 and 42% in 1932-36. Today's stock returns (28% over 1995-99) are in line with those of the past. Although economic growth is reasonably fast now, we would need to see two more years of 6%+ GDP growth for a fifty-year peacetime record to be set now. Perhaps we will still see it, the strength of current GDP growth at such a late stage in such a long expansion suggests that the economy is trying to follow the Kondratiev script. But with the Federal reserve in hiking mode, the dangerously overvalued equity markets, and high degree of debt, we probably won't set a record this time. Nevertheless, the strong economy of today is consistent with our putative position within the Kondratiev cycle.

Figure 5.6 Growth rates in nominal GDP per capita during downwaves

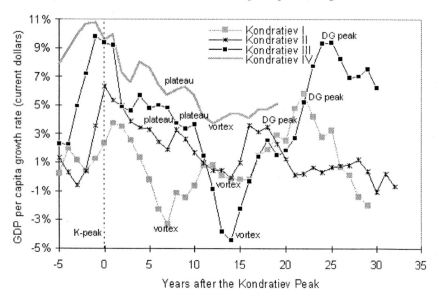

Table 5.3 shows specific dates for the features shown in Figures 5.5 and 5.6. Corresponding dates from the stock index are shown as well. We can use the spacing from each signpost (K-peak, plateau, Vortex) to the DG-peak for each of the three previous cycles to obtain estimates for when the DG peak might appear during this cycle. For example, on a price basis, the DG-peak occurred 22 years after the K-peak in the first cycle, 16 years after the K-peak in the second cycle and 17 years after the K-peak in the third cycle. If we add these values to the K-peak for the current cycle (1980) we obtain three estimates for the coming DG-peak: 2002, 1996, and 1997. We can use the spacing between the DG-peak and the plateau in the same way to obtain three more estimates for when the DG peak might appear. Finally we can use the spacing between the DG-peak and the vortex. In this way nine estimates for the DG peak were obtained, which were averaged together to obtain a consensus. For price/inflation the consensus DG-peak is 2002 ± 4. For GDP the consensus DG-peak is 2001 ± 4. For the stock index, the consensus value is 1999 ± 5. The same analysis was performed for the K-trough. Values of 2013 ± 3, 2010 ± 3, 2011 ± 3 were obtained for prices, GDP and stocks, respectively. These values appear in Table 5.3.

Summary and Conclusions

The Kondratiev cycle was presented in terms of prices. Historical price data was used to show the cycles explicitly for the U.S and British economies. The idea of fluctuating real economic performance was shown as apparent cycles in GDP around its long-term trend. We saw how the combination of the Kuznets cycle and Kondratiev cycle produces a repeating sequence of "economic seasons" that produce the secular bear and bull markets. Finally we saw how the detailed economic characteristics of past cycles corresponds well with the economic characteristics exhibited by the economy now. Extending the analogy we found that the most likely time for the bull market to end is between now and 2004. This prediction is consistent with the historically-high value of P/R today.

Table 5.3. Dates for Kondratiev signposts in terms of Price,
GDP per capita and the Stock Index

	Feature	K-peak	Plateau	Vortex	DG-peak	K-trough
Kondratiev I **(1787-1843)**	Price	1814	1818	1829	1836	1843
	GDP per capita	1816	--	1821	1836	1843
	Stock	1815	1818	1819	1835	1843
Kondratiev II **(1843-1897)**	Price	1864	1872	1878	1882	1897
	GDP per capita	1864	1872	1878	1882	1896
	Stock	1861	1872	1877	1881	1896
Kondratiev **(1897-1949)**	Price	1919	1925	1932	1937	1949
	GDP per capita	1920	1929	1933	1944	1949
	Stock	1921	1929	1932	1937	1949
Kondratiev **(1949-**	Price	1980	1990	1998	2002 ± 4	2013 ± 3
	GDP per capita	1979	1989	1992	2001 ± 4	2010 ± 3
	Stock	1982	1987	1990	1999 ± 5	2011 ± 3

Historical cycle-based analysis, whether of stocks (P/R) or of the economy (Kondratiev cycle) paints a pretty intriguing picture. But it is a picture of correlation and analogies. We have no proven mechanism that explains why there is a Kondratiev cycle or how it works. Most economists acknowledge that semi-regular fluctuations in price levels have occurred in the past, but there is no consensus as to whether semi-regular fluctuations in economic growth have ever occurred, much less are operative today.

The purpose of my presentation of the Kondratiev cycle is to recast the idea of stock cycles (something that has not received much study) in terms of economic cycles that have been studied by professional social scientists. Tapping into the rich literature on long cycles, evidence can be assembled to make the case for a Kondratiev cycle. This case is strengthened by the addition of the parallel stock cycle, which adds a second line of support for the largely price-defined Kondratiev cycle.

The lack of a mechanism weakens the argument for the Kondratiev cycle. The calendar was used successfully for millennia before the mechanism behind it was discovered, however. The absence of a mechanism did not make the calendar any less valid. On the other hand, there were hundreds of observations of the calendar cycle, all of which showed it to be of precisely the same length, as opposed to just three U.S. Kondratiev cycles of variable length. The situation with stock/Kondratiev cycles is more similar to the situation for astrology than the calendar. Had we more cycles, or additional economic variables that align with the existing cycles, our confidence in the validity of these cycles would be enhanced.

Table 5.1 shows that we do have nearly a dozen incidences of the Kondratiev cycle, but the pre-1800 cycles are not well-characterized. We don't have GDP data before 1790 or U.S. stock data from before 1802. We do have real wages, an index of industrial production and annual stock index prices for the British economy in the 18th century. Eighteenth century British stock prices simply reflected interest rates; they peaked when interest rates troughed and vice-versa. Hence they gave no additional information other than that already present in the interest rate data—which we have already used to characterize the 18th century Kondratiev cycle. Real wages simply reflected the price situation, and also provide no additional information. Industrial production shows a biphasic growth pattern with a shift from a low rate to a high one right around 1780, corresponding to the onset of the Industrial Revolution. Without the supporting evidence of GDP and stock cycles for the post-1790 U.S. economy it is hard to be sure that the putative Kondratiev cycles before 1790 are the same thing as those seen afterward, which we are using to support our forecast of a secular bear market. Many economists who study long cycles, including Kondratiev himself, maintain that they only apply to the period after the industrial revolution.

If we could find an additional, independent characteristic that correlates with the Kondratiev cycle both before and after 1790 we could then use the pre-industrial Kondratiev cycles as additional examples of the operation of the Kondratiev cycle, strengthening our confidence that they are a real phenomenon.

In the next chapter we will explore the idea that each Kondratiev cycle creates a "new economy" as it unfolds, and that the information economy of today is simply the fourth new economy in the U.S. since the start of the industrial revolution. I will also extend this idea of new economies to the pre-industrial period to support the contention that all the Kondratiev cycles shown in Table 5.1 represent the same recurrent phenomenon.

Chapter Six

The Innovation Wave

The Harvard economist Joseph Schumpeter attempted to build a theory[22] for the Kondratiev cycle, or longwave, as we will refer to it here. His view was that the longwave reflected the impact of concentrated bursts of innovation that transformed the economy. He coined the term "creative destruction" to describe how the creation of new industries and superior business methods in existing industries partially replaced (destroyed) old industries and methods. These new industries and methods can be described as a "new economy" that both adds to and partially replaces the old one. The development of a new economy creates new areas of economic activity that did not exist previously. These new areas can then grow strongly for decades as they spread into every part of the economy. This growth can occur readily because resources formerly employed by the old economy are freed up by productivity enhancements resulting from the adoption of new methods. The period during which this replacement takes place is the Kondratiev downwave.

Schumpeter's writings are rather difficult to follow. Since his time, his ideas have been extended and formulated in different ways by a number of researchers. Gerhard Mensch[23] has developed a more explicit model for Schumpeterian innovation that fits an *innovation wave* into the longwave. The business consultant and popular financial writer Harry Dent[24] describes a four-step economic cycle that is similar to Mensch's model for the longwave, but with a number of new twists. In this chapter we will develop our own version of the innovation wave. We will use Dent's terminology and conceptual scheme as it is easy to

113

understand, but will come up with a somewhat different detailed for-mulation, and will use it to reach different conclusions.

The purpose of this effort is to establish a second, non-monetary characterization of the longwave. If successful we will have two, largely independent, periodic phenomenon that we can use to characterize the changing economic environment that brings about the stock cycle. This will strengthen the possibility that the longwave is real. It will also give us a historical handle on the "new economy" of today which will help us decide whether or not the Internet phenomenon is really all that new.

The Product Innovation Cycle

New products and technologies typically go through three stages of growth: an innovation phase, a growth phase and a maturity phase. These three stages are shown graphically by what is called the *logistics* or S-curve (see Figure 6.1). A key property of the logistics curve is that it takes about the same time for market penetration to go from 1% to 10%, 10% to 50%, and 50% to 90%. Dent defines the period during which penetration increases from zero to 10% as the innovation phase of the S-curve. The period from 10% to 90% penetration is called the growth period. Finally the period from 90% and up is termed the maturity period.

The Innovation Cycle for the Economy

Dent extends the S-curve concept to the entire economy. He notes that some periods are richer in entrepreneurial activity than others. One such period was around 1900, when many of the common mass-market brand-name products like Gillette® razors, Coca-Cola® or Ford® automobiles were introduced. Following Mensch, Dent calls the inno-vations associated with these entrepreneurial periods "basic innova-tions" because they form the base for a new economy. He calls periods when the basic innovations appear the innovation phase for the new economy. The period around 1900 would then be the innovation phase for the "mass-market" economy.

Figure 6.1. The logistics or S-curve

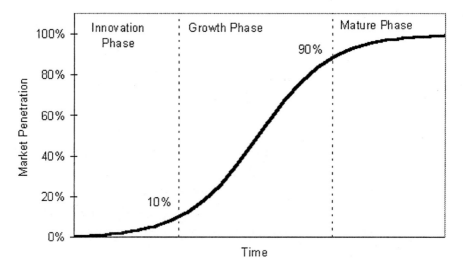

Initially, the basic innovations operate on the margins of the old economy. Gradually, they are adopted by a small, but significant, fraction of the economy. At this point, the new economy enters its growth phase, during which the basic innovations move into the mainstream. Thus far, the development of the new economy follows the same S-curve as does the development of an individual product or technology with an innovation period (0-10% adoption) followed by a growth phase (10-90% adoption). Dent calls this growth phase the growth boom of the new economy.

The next phase of the developing economy is the shakeout. The shakeout occurs when many firms, attracted by the opportunities of the growth phase, enter the business and encounter increased competition as the market becomes saturated. Saturation results in increased price competition and business failures. The shakeout is a period of deflation and depression. It is also a period of innovation, but of a different sort.

During the shakeout, new technologies and products are developed that complement and improve upon the basic innovations. Dent calls these "maturity innovations". Of the many new-economy companies that existed at the end of the growth period, only a few successfully employ the complementary maturity innovations and products to win the competition and survive the shakeout. Following the shakeout, a new growth period begins, during which improved versions of otherwise mature products are sold. This period is called the maturity boom.

Another way of describing the maturity boom is the growth phase of the mature-type innovations. In this concept the shakeout is the overlap of the basic innovation's mature phase and the mature innovation's innovation phase. Figure 6.2 shows a diagram of this idea. The S-curves for the basic and maturity innovations are combined into a composite "double-S" curve that we will call the innovation wave.

Figure 6.2 Diagram of Dent's Innovation Cycle

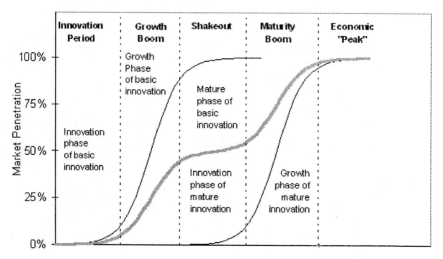

Detailed assignment of historical innovation wave to the mass-market economy

We will start with what Dent called the mass-market economy that got its start around 1900 as described earlier. He implies that there was a growth boom during the 1910's and 1920's that was associated with what he calls "the Henry Ford generation" and a maturity boom from the late 1940's to late 1960's that was associated with what he calls "the Bob Hope generation". Although he introduces the concepts of the S-curve and the "four stroke" economic cycle, he never explicitly applies it to past economies. We will try to do so here.

First we identify industries that became important during the first three quarters of the 20th century. The scheme shown in Figure 6.2 can then be applied by compiling S-curve data for these industries. The market penetration for a particular product can be expressed as units possessed or consumed per household or worker. Alternately, the growth in importance of a new industry, measured in terms of units of output per unit of GDP, can be used as a measure of extent of growth or "penetration" into the economy. Labor force data describing what fraction of the workforce is engaged in a particular new activity might also be expected to show some sort of innovation wave. Once a number of innovation waves for industries characteristic of a particular economy have been obtained, they can be averaged together to produce a composite innovation wave that defines that economy. The growth boom and maturity boom are obtained by analogy to Figure 6.2. By looking at the timing of the basic innovations underlying that economy, an estimate for the innovation period can be obtained as well. We will start by applying these ideas to a couple of single industries. Then we will move on to entire economies.

Our first example is broadcasting. Broadcasting started with the development of voice radio transmissions in the 1906-1917 period. The first radio station went on the air in 1917 and the dominant radio company of the era, Radio Corporation of America (RCA), was spun off from General Electric in 1919. RCA and others developed television during the 1926-1939 period. The first US television station went on the air in 1939 and the first major television network (NBC) was established by RCA in 1941. A second wave of growth in broadcasting got underway after this. Figure 6.3 documents this entire process by showing the growth in the percentage of households with radio and television sets over the 1922-1995 period. We see growth curves for radio and television that strongly resemble Figure 6.2. In Dent's terminology, radio would be the basic innovation and television would be the maturity innovation. If we average the two curves together we get the broadcasting innovation wave, which shows an initial growth period up to around 1940, a flat period to 1946 and then resumption of the trend upwards to a peak in 1970. By analogy to Figure 6.2, we denote the radio growth phase as the growth boom (1925-1940) and the television growth phase as the maturity boom (1946-1970). The flat period in the composite curve (1940-46) becomes the shakeout. By analogy with Figure 6.1, I identified 1925 as the beginning of the growth boom, since that is when the composite growth curve reached 10% of its 1940 level.

Figure 6.3. The innovation wave for the radio and television

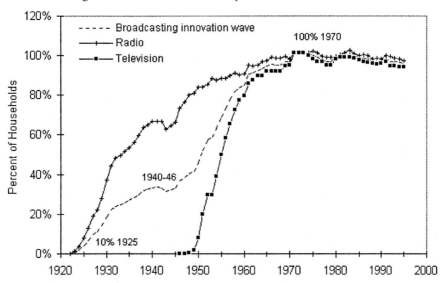

We now try to apply this idea to the auto industry. Figure 6.4 shows two kinds of growth curves. The first is a plot of the total automobile fleet divided by the labor force. This shows the growth of the auto in terms of market penetration. This curve is shaped much like the prototypical innovation wave in Figure 6.2. There is a definite growth boom up to 1929, a shakeout from 1929 to 1949 and a maturity boom from 1949 to 1973. Unlike with radio and TV, where the basic and maturity innovations reflect distinct products, in the case of the auto, the maturity innovations included such things as the automatic transmission, power features and the interstate system, which made using a car for personal transportation more appealing to a broader spectrum of the public.

The second curve in Figure 6.4 shows the annual production of vehicles per million (constant) dollars of GDP. This ratio indicates the importance of the auto industry relative to the economy as a whole. As a major economic element, the auto industry peaked in the 1920's. The initial growth in the auto industry reflects the growth boom in market penetration. We can date the beginning of this growth boom as the point when production of cars reached 10% of the importance it would have at the growth boom peak in 1929. Thus, we would date the growth boom for the auto as 1907-1929, the shakeout from 1929-1949 and the maturity boom from 1949-1973.

Figure 6.4. The innovation wave for the automobile

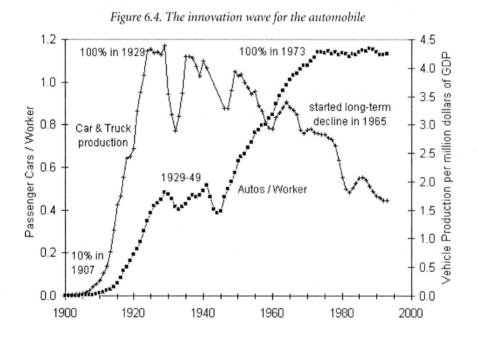

These examples illustrate the use of market-penetration and production-volume curves. Market penetration curves are those that measure the extent to which the innovation has saturated a market. The broadcasting innovation wave is of this type. Volume curves use the levels of physical output relative to GDP (in constant dollars) as a measure of the extent to which the new economic activity has diffused throughout the economy. It measures the economic penetration of a new innovation (or cluster of innovations). To apply this graphical analysis to a whole new economy we obtain as many curves of either sort as we can for important industries in that economy and average them together to produce composite market and economic penetration curves. These curves are then inspected to obtain the dates of the growth boom, shakeout and maturity boom.

Innovation waves were constructed for nine industries and estimates for growth and maturity booms obtained (see Table 6.1). Production volume data were averaged together to form a composite output curve. Similarly, market penetration data were averaged into a composite innovation wave. Both curves are shown in Figure 6.5.

The US aircraft industry got its start in 1909 with the founding of the Wright Aeronautical Corporation. Early growth was slow; subsidies by the US government for airmail deliveries were largely responsible for keeping the industry alive until the mid 1930's. With the development of the DC-3 and the stimulus of WW II, the air travel industry grew tremendously. Passenger flights per worker were used as a measure of market extent and appear in the composite market penetration curve in Figure 6.5. Passenger air-miles per unit of GDP were used as a measure of economic penetration and appear in the composite output curve. Growth in flights per worker appears to have leveled off after 1987. This date is used for the end of the maturity boom in Table 6.1. There is no clear interruption in either curve that signifies a shakeout. Hence the date of 50% extent is used in its place.

The growth in high school education during the mass-market economy is used as an example of penetration of a "social innovation" into the population brought about by economic development during the mass-market economy. It reached "market saturation" in terms of the fraction of the 14-18 age cohort attending high school in around 1970. Like the airline industry, education shows no shakeout (one wouldn't expect it to). The 50% extent date is used in place of a shakeout.

Table 6.1. Mass-market economy industries

Industry	Innovation Date	Growth Boom	Maturity Boom
Airline	1909	1951-1967	1967-1987
Broadcasting	1917	1925-1940	1946-1970
Education (Secondary)	--	1910-1940	1940-1970
Electric Power	1882	1905-1941	1945-1976
Electric Appliances	1901	1909-1937	1943-1960
Motor Vehicles	1893	1907-1929	1949-1973
Petroleum	1859	1889-1937	1943-1956
Synthetic Fibers	1884	1921-1936	1943-1978
Telephone	1876	1907-1929	1945-1980
Composite	**1895**	**1908-1937**	**1944-1973**

The electric power generation industry got its start with Edison's establishment of the Pearl Street electric generating station in 1882. Growth of this industry was measured as kilowatt-hours of power generated per unit of GDP and appears in the composite output curve. We can interpret the period of initial buildout by both public and private utilities (largely in urban areas) as the growth boom. The rural electrification programs of the 1930's and 1940's brought electric power to a previously underserved population. The availability of cheap power and good roads in rural areas led to the movement of industry out of crowded multistory urban facilities and into spacious single-story rural facilities. These newer facilities were designed to maximize efficiency and to allow for easy expansion by removing the constraints imposed by the crowded urban environment. This development encouraged enormous expansion in electrical power generation and use in the post-war years (and strong growth in industrial and manufacturing industries). The 1930's and 1940's electrification programs and the new industrial model can be thought of as maturity innovations, and the strong post-war growth in electrical generation as the maturity boom for the electric power industry. The electric appliance industry, quite naturally, follows the growth of electricity. The number of major electric appliances (refrigerators, stoves and washing machines) per worker reached a plateau after 1960, implying market saturation.

The petroleum industry is the earliest appearing industry in Table 6.1. Its growth was measured in terms of barrels of crude oil consumed per unit of GDP. The timing of the innovation of the oil well in 1859, and the start of the growth boom in 1882 suggest that petroleum might belong in an earlier economy. Indeed, in its origin, petroleum was a fairly minor industry that mostly provided a replacement for whale oil in lamps. Had the auto not come along, the petroleum industry would have remained a minor player from an earlier economy. With the development of the automobile an additional market for its products was created, which soon outstripped all others. In time the petroleum industry grew into a dominant industry, and spawned a new industry, the petrochemical industry, as sort of a maturity innovation.

I couldn't find data series on petrochemicals, but I did find some on artificial and synthetic fibers. Growth of these was measured in terms of pounds produced per unit of GDP. Late in the 19th century, the chemical industry developed artificial fibers such as rayon and cellulose acetate. By World War II these materials had reached their apex of importance. Around this time, completely synthetic polymers such as nylon and polyester were introduced which further expanded the industry. Synthetic fibers continued to grow in importance until the 1970's. Along with the synthetic fibers came plastics like polystyrene

(Styrofoam) and a host of petrochemicals, derived from natural gas or petroleum. The whole development of the synthetic materials and petrochemical industry can be considered as a maturity innovation by the chemical and petroleum industries, allowing existing firms to expand into new markets.

Finally there was the telephone industry. Like electric power, the growth of telephony required substantial infrastructure and proceeded slowly at first. The growth of the telephone showed both growth and maturity booms that might have reflected some of the same factors as did electric power (e.g. extension into rural areas).

The composite profiles appear in Figure 6.5. These curves show the growth of the mass-market economy in terms of both output (economic penetration) and market penetration. The output curve shows a broad top in 1973-1979 after which it starts to decline. The market penetration curve shows a plateau after 1973 indicating that the mass production economy industries as a whole saturated their markets after 1973. With these observations, we would put the "economic peak" or end of the maturity boom of the mass-market economy in 1973. The output curve shows a dip from 1937 to 1944 that can be interpreted as the shakeout, making 1944-1973 the maturity boom. For the start of the growth boom we use 1908, when economic penetration reached 10% of the 1937 level.

Thus far there has been no discussion of the innovation period. By Dent's construction, the innovation period ends when the growth boom began in 1908. Since we employed average growth curves to obtain the other periods, we average the innovation dates in Table 6.1 to estimate the center of the innovation period. The average of these dates is 1895, which we will denote as the center of the mass production innovation wave. This gives dates for the innovation period as 1882-1908.

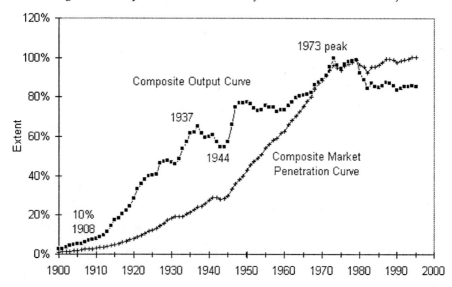

Figure 6.5 Composite innovation waves for the mass-market economy

Note that the first oil well (1859) is not counted as a mass-market innovation. The growth in oil consumption associated with the growth of the mass-market economy was not brought about by the development of oil drilling, but rather, by the innovation of new products and services like automobiles and air travel that created a huge market for oil, while creating vibrant new industries in their own right. The innovation of oil drilling was not counted as a basic innovation for the mass-market economy since it did not create its own growth dynamic.

Application of the innovation wave to older economies

The stocks of firms that deal with the goods and services of the mass-market economy today are typified as stodgy "old economy" Dow stocks like GM in order to distinguish them from the red-hot "new economy" NASDAQ stocks like Yahoo. It has become apparent to investors and market commentators that there is a new "information economy" growing on top of the old one and this shows up in the performance of the old versus new-economy stocks. Let us now go back to the 1920's when the Dow Industrials contained red-hots like RCA and the stodgy companies filled the Rails index. In those days it would be the hot new mass-market economy that would be compared to an old "railroad economy". And the difference showed up in the performance of their respective indices. The Dow Industrials crushed the Rails in the 1920's, just as today the NASDAQ leaves the Dow Industrials in the dust. So now we will analyze the "railroad economy" that was associated with these rail stocks in the same way as we proceeded with Dent's mass-market economy. Dent never mentioned an economy prior to the mass-market economy, so we are treading new ground here.

Table 6.2 shows that the key industries of this economy are represented by the railroads, the coal industry, the iron & steel industry, the telegraph industry and elementary school education. The growth of the railroad industry was measured in terms of ton miles of freight shipped per unit of GDP. Growth of the coal, iron and steel industry was measured as tons of each produced per unit of GDP. The number of telegrams sent per unit of GDP was used as a measure of the changing importance of the telegraph industry over time. Growth of public school education was measured as the fraction of the school-aged population that attended school.

Table 6.2. Railroad/industrial economy industries

Industry	Innovation Date	Growth Boom	Maturity Boom
Coal	--	1844-1883	1883-1917
Education (Elementary)	--	-1851	1851-1930
Iron	--	1846-1889	1889-1916
Railroad	1830	1857-1887	1887-1917
Steel	1855	1878-1898	1898-1918
Telegraph	1844	1860-1893	1906-1929
Composite	**1839**	**1847-1889**	**1895-1917**

The first railroad was established in the US in 1830. Ton-miles shipped steadily rose until it peaked (relative to GDP) during World War I. The iron industry grew steadily with the railroads, and later, the steel industry too. So did the coal industry. All three reached their peak during WW I along with the railroads. We note that both the coal and the iron industries were already long established at the beginning of the railroad period; they do not represent basic innovations for the railroad/industrial economy. The coal and iron industries did not create their own growth dynamic. Instead, they piggybacked on the growth of the railroads, much as oil did on the automobile. They were included in the railroad/industrial economy because they reached their maximum in importance to the economy at the same time as the railroads. On the other hand, the development of steel can be considered as a late basic innovation in response to the need for a better structural metal for the burgeoning railroad/industrial economy, and therefore, it produced its own growth dynamic. The data in Table 6.2 was combined into a composite curve for the railroad/industrial economy and is shown in Figure

6.6. An interruption in growth is seen in 1888-1895, which we label the shakeout. The extent of the economy reached 10% of its 1888 level in 1847, allowing assignment of 1847-1888 for the growth boom. The maturity boom then falls into the 1895-1917 period. Proceeding as before, we average the innovation dates in Table 6.2 to obtain 1839, which serves as the center for the 1831-1847 innovation period.

Although the number of industries employed is smaller than those used for the mass-market economy, we still have representatives for most of the important categories examined in the mass-market case (transportation, education, energy, communications and basic materials) so the analysis is still reasonably comprehensive. There are some interesting differences. Mature growth for the railroad/industrial economy was obtained by incremental innovations in existing products (e.g. the air brake and refrigerated railroad car) and a wave of industry consolidations around the time of the shakeout that led to greater efficiency and greater pricing power. Although incremental innovations (e.g. automatic transmissions) and consolidations also occurred during the shakeout of the mass-market economy, that wasn't the whole story. A slew of new products (e.g. television over radio, polyester over rayon) contributed to the mature growth of the mass-market economy. The combined effect of new products plus improved versions of old products and industry consolidation gave the mass-market economy a longer and stronger maturity boom than occurred for the railroad/industrial economy.

Figure 6.6 Composite S-curve for the railroad/industrial Economy (1830-1945)

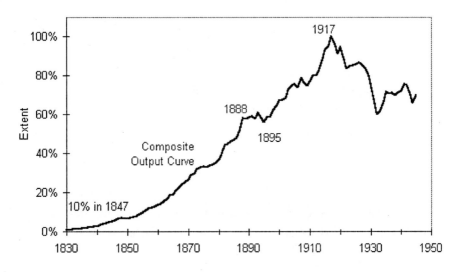

The economy before the railroad/industrial economy I call the cotton/textile economy. The driver for this economy's growth was the existence of a vast foreign market whose exploitation was made possible by a key innovation. Textiles were a key growth industry associated with the Industrial Revolution in Great Britain. Strong growth of textile production gave rise to a rapidly growing demand for fiber during the second half of the eighteenth century. Cotton is an excellent fiber for use in textiles, and it was well suited to the climate of the southern half of the United States. This combination created the potential for development of a major cotton industry in the US to feed the British demand. The hitch was that removal of the cotton fibers from the seeds was very labor-intensive and so the costs of production made growing cotton unattractive. Relatively little cotton was planted during most of the 18th century—tobacco was the principal cash crop. This situation suddenly changed in 1793 when Eli Whitney filed a patent for his cotton engine or "cotton gin". This device readily separated the cotton fibers from the seeds, making cotton production very attractive. Cotton production exploded and a new economy was born.

The only relevant data I could find were annual cotton production volumes and prices, decennial estimates of the size of the textile workforce and inland water traffic on New York State canals. All of these are plotted in Figure 6.7. Although data for coal and iron production are available, the major growth of these industries occurred later, during the railroad economy. In contrast, the growth of the cotton industry was enormous at this time. So the cotton industry became the defining industry for a new cotton/textile economy which was made possible by the basic innovation of the cotton gin.

Figure 6.7 Production and labor force data for the cotton/textile economy (1790-1900)

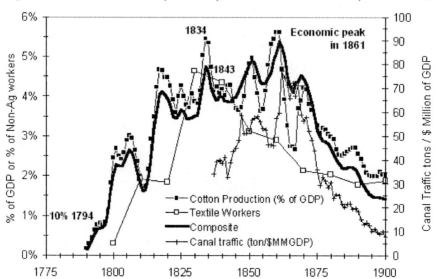

Figure 6.7 shows the growth of cotton and textiles as major components of the economy. The value of cotton produced grew from only 0.2% of the GDP in 1790 to about 5.5% by the mid 1830's. After this it remained roughly at this level for about 25 years and then declined in importance. The textile industry began to develop in the United States after 1790 as well. The importance of the textile industry shows a similar initial growth trend. In terms of the fraction of the non-agricultural workforce employed, textiles grew from 0.3% to nearly 5% in the 1830's, falling off afterward. Also shown is canal traffic in tons per million dollars of GDP for the years after 1837. A composite of the cotton production and canal traffic curves is shown, which was used to date the cotton/textile economy.

The 1834 peak in cotton production, when cotton reached maximum importance to the economy, was used to denote the end of the growth boom. This peak is consistent with the peak in textile workers as a percentage of the labor force. The slump from 1834 to 1843 in the composite curve is the shakeout and the secondary rise from 1843 to 1861 becomes the maturity boom. The growth boom begins when the first growth phase reaches 10% of its peak value. Cotton production (relative to GDP) reached 10% of its 1834 peak value in 1794. Hence, we can interpret the 1794-1834 period as the growth boom.

The cotton/textile economy was not an internally-generated new economy. Its success reflected the strong market in Great Britain. Hence, we should look for the origins of this economy in the cluster of British textile innovations in the late 18th century (e.g. spinning jenny 1764, water frame 1769, water mule 1779, and power loom 1785) as well as the cotton gin itself. In this sense the cotton gin can be considered as just the last of many important innovations that lead to the development of the textile economy in Great Britain and the cotton/textile economy in the United States. The average of these innovation dates is 1778, which gives the innovation period as 1762-1794.

Figure 6.8. Data for shipping and agricultural industries 1789-1900

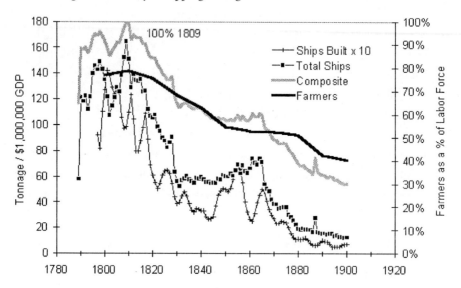

Going back still further, we can look at the pre-industrial US economy that existed before the establishment of the first textile mill in the US or the invention of the cotton gin. I call this economy the Agricultural/Commerce Economy, reflecting two major industries, farming and trade (shipping). Figure 6.8 shows a graph of information concerning this early economy. The fraction of the US labor force that were farmers is shown as a measure of the importance of the agricultural economy. Also shown is the total tonnage of the US merchant fleet and the tonnage constructed per million dollars of GDP. We see that the relative importance of shipping peaked around 1809, possibly reflecting the cessation of the slave trade in 1807, or growing tensions with Great Britain, a major trading partner. The War of 1812 naturally disrupted Anglo-American trade, a mainstay of the commerce economy. After the war, the American shipping/commerce industry never regained its pre-war importance, probably because of the growing importance of the burgeoning cotton/textile economy. The importance of agriculture also started to decline after 1810. A composite curve is shown which suggests that the agriculture/commerce economy reached its economic peak around 1809.

Today's Economy

Today's new economy is the information/networked economy, or just information economy. Unlike the previous economies, which were characterized by the appearance of a wide range of startling consumer products and services (e.g. cars, broadcasting, air travel), the information economy deals with a more intangible "product": information management and knowledge production. Information management includes activities such as supply chain management, product inventory control, marketing, and distribution. Products that serve information management needs include communications products (e.g. cellular phones, the Internet) and information technology (IT) products (computers, software, embedded chips). Knowledge production includes such things as drug discovery research at pharmaceutical and biotech companies, and research carried out at research universities and private research institutions.

Figure 6.9 Information economy market penetration curves

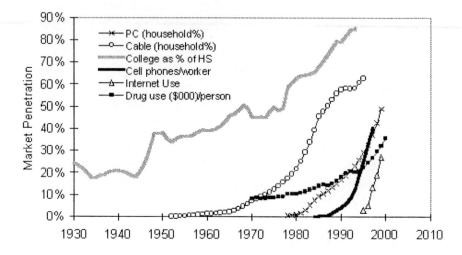

To track the growth of the information economy I selected eight industries, three in communications, three in information technology and two in the knowledge business. Market penetration data is shown in Figure 6.9 while economic penetration data is shown in Figure 6.10. Communications forms the backbone for the developing information economy. Three examples from the communications industry were chosen as measures for this economy: the growth of the cable television network; the growth of cellular phones; and the Internet. Cable shows the development of what will soon become a high-speed data network linking American (and world) households and is tracked in Figure 6.9 as the growth in the fraction of American households with cable. Cellular phones shows the development of portable communications devices, which serve to link individuals when they are away from their home or office "base". It was tracked in Figure 6.9 by the growth in the percentage of workers with cell phones and in Figure 6.10 by the growth in cellular revenues as a percentage of GDP. Lastly, the growth in the (mostly low speed) Internet shows the development of a data-transmission culture linking households, businesses, and individuals. It was tracked by the growth in the percentage of U.S. households with Internet access.

In addition to communications (the ability to exchange information) participants in the new economy must be able to manage this information. Hence information technology (IT) is also a leading sector in the new economy. The growth in personal computers (PCs) both in terms of the fraction of U.S. households with a PC (Figure 6.9) and the amount of PC sales as a percentage of GDP (Figure 6.10) were used to track this important aspect of IT growth. The growth of the semiconductor and software industry as a fraction of GDP are shown in Figure 6.10 as two additional measures of IT growth. Drug discovery research was included as one example of a knowledge industry and appears in Figure 6.10. The development of the information economy requires not only new communications and information-processing technologies, but also a new kind of information-savvy worker. The growth in college-level education (Figure 6.9) is shown to track the appearance of this information-savvy worker and as another example of a knowledge industry.

Figure 6.10. Information economy economic penetration curves

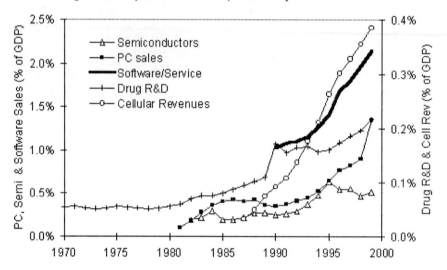

Figure 6.9 shows market penetration curves for the PC, Internet, cellular phone, cable and pharmaceutical consumption. Also shown is the growth in college attendance, expressed as a ratio of college students to high school students, each relative to their respective age cohorts. Figure 6.10 shows economic penetration curves for PC, software, and semiconductor sales, drug discovery research, and cellular phone revenues. Composite curves based on market and economic extent were produced from the data in Figures 6.9 and 6.10, respectively. They are shown in Figure 6.11. The market penetration curve reached the 10% threshold in 1980 providing one measure for the start of the growth boom (see Figure 6.1). The sudden takeoff of the economic curve suggests 1981 or 1982. I chose 1981 as the consensus value.

Using innovation data: the integrated circuit (1958) and the founding of Intel (1968) for semiconductors, the Arapanet and Unix operating system (1969) for the Internet, the PC (1974) and the founding of Apple (1976) for the PC, genetic engineering (1976) for drug research, and the founding of Microsoft (1977) for software we get an average value of 1971 for the cluster of innovations leading to the information economy. The period 1961-1981 was selected as the innovation period as it was centered on 1971 and ended when the growth boom began in 1981.

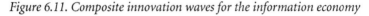

Figure 6.11. Composite innovation waves for the information economy

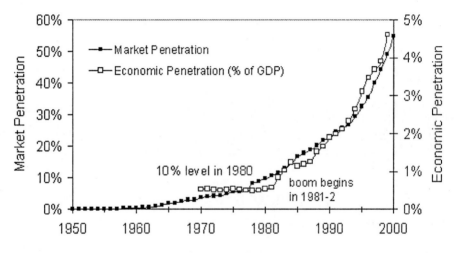

Correspondence between the innovation wave and the longwave

Table 6.3 summarizes the Dentian phases for the five economies just discussed. The average length of each economy is about 90 years. Since they overlap, the spacing between each economy is less. The cotton/textile economy followed the Agricultural/Commerce economy by 52 years. The railroad cycle followed the cotton cycle by 55 years. The mass production economy followed the railroad economy by 53 years. On average, these cycles are spaced 53 years apart, a value close to the average length of the post-1790 longwave. Inspection of the "economic peaks" (the end of the maturity boom) shows that they occur 2-7 years before K-peaks. There is also a correspondence between the beginning of the maturity boom and the K-trough. That is, the maturity boom appears to be correlated with the upwave. Innovation waves appear to be generated at a Kondratiev frequency. That is, they are generated and grow in such a way so that their ultimate peaks occur just before a K-peak.

Table 6.3 Dates for the four phases of the innovations cycle from previous cycles

Economy	Innovation	Growth Boom	Shakeout	Maturity Boom
Agricultural / Commerce	--	--	--	-1809
Cotton / Textile	1762-1794	1794-1834	1834-1843	1843-1861
Railroad / Industrial	1831-1847	1847-1888	1888-1895	1895-1917
Mass Production	1882-1908	1908-1937	1937-1944	1944-1973
Information	1961-1981	1981-2007?	2007-2014?	--

Leading Sectors of the World Economy

Modelski and Thompson[25] wrote an intriguing interpretation of history as a global world system in which successive powers emerge as the leading nations of their time. Prior to their emergence these powers pioneer new leading sectors of the world economy. Each of these leading sectors appears to be the same thing as what I have been calling a "new economy" or the innovation wave. There is a fundamental innovation, which could be discovery of new lands/markets, development of new crops or products for trade, or the opening up of existing markets that had previously been closed. These innovations give birth to a new leading sector, just as a cluster of new basic innovations give rise to a new economy. Successful exploitation of this sector by one of the innovating powers results in that power becoming the leading nation of the (Western) world. Since 1500, according to Modelski, there have been four leading powers: Portugal, the Netherlands, Great Britain and the United States.

Consider the rising European states at the end of the Middle ages. In those days wars were fought mostly with mercenaries and so national power was directly dependent on the ability of the nation to raise cash to pay mercenaries. A readily available source of cash was taxes on trade. So national power depended, in part, on the extent and profitability of trade. The most profitable trade was with India and the Far East, in which European gold and silver were exchanged for Asian spices. During the Middle Ages this trade was routed through the Italian city-states of Venice and Genoa, who reaped the lion's share of the profits. Not surprisingly, Western European nations were very interested in finding a way to tap into these riches.

There were two potential strategies to do this: (1) find a cheap source of gold or silver for exchange through the existing Italian-controlled route, or (2) find an alternate route to India and circumvent the Italian middlemen. In 1415 and afterward, Portugal attempted to achieve the first of these by trying to seize Moroccan ports and so muscle themselves into the Saharan gold trade. Morocco proved difficult to conquer, so Portugal tried sailing south along the African coast in an effort to go directly to the source of the gold and bypass the Muslim intermediaries. They succeeded in doing this around the middle of the century. This accomplishment constitutes an innovation that launched a new economy (what Modelski calls a leading sector). Figure 6.12 shows the leading sectors as a series of innovation waves. The first of these is importation of Guinea Gold by Portugal.

The Portuguese exploration continued south along the African coast, reaching the Cape of Good Hope in 1488 and India in 1497. Meanwhile, Christopher Columbus, an Italian sea captain in the employ of Spain, discovered the New World in 1492. These discoveries constitute a new set of innovations which led to Portuguese domination of the spice trade and to a Spanish monopoly on American gold and silver. Spanish importation of gold and (later) silver from the New World helped fund Spain's bid for European mastery (1519-1659).[26] The second wave in Figure 6.12 shows the Portuguese Pepper/Spanish Gold leading sector.

As the 16th century progressed, the Portuguese established trading bases throughout South Asia and the East Indies. When the Guinea gold trade dried up, the Portuguese branched into slaves, establishing extensive sugar plantations in Brazil. Distribution of Portuguese pepper and Spanish silver in exchange for needed naval stores and other goods occurred at Dutch ports on the Baltic. This was necessary because of the central location of the Netherlands relative to Portugal and Spain on one side and Scandinavian naval stores and East European agricultural products on the other. As the Portuguese grew rich from their Asian trade, the Dutch developed into the leading trading nation on the Baltic. This was achieved partly because of their strategic location, but also because of Dutch naval innovations such as the development of the fluyt in the mid-16th century. A fluyt is a trading ship that required 20% less crew than other ships of the time. Since labor dominates trading costs this development gave Dutch traders a big edge over their rivals. Also at this time, the discovery of the Potosi silver mine in 1544 made large quantities of South American silver available to Spain. Thus, the third leading sector wave was Portuguese sugar and Asian trade, Dutch Baltic trade and Spanish silver.

For most of the sixteenth century, the Netherlands was a Spanish possession. As their prosperity grew, the Dutch chafed under Spanish rule and finally revolted in 1572, driving out the Spanish garrisons in 1576 and declaring independence in 1581. Spain was forced to concede defeat by 1609. In 1580, Spain gained control of Portugal, and blocked Dutch access to Portuguese Asian Trade. The Dutch resolved to circumvent the Portuguese and go directly to the source for their Asian wares. One by one the Dutch captured the Portuguese Asian outposts, gradually eroding the Portuguese Asian trade monopoly. The next (fourth) leading sector was this growth in Dutch Asian trade.

Figure 6.12. Innovation waves (leading sectors) since the 15th century

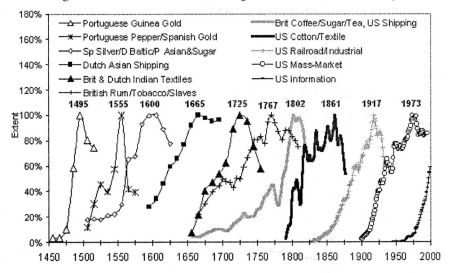

Meanwhile the British were also moving into the Asian trade business at Portuguese expense. They formed their own East India company at about the same time as the Dutch did. The next (fifth) wave had the British overtaking the Dutch in the Indian textile business and the Dutch displacing the Portuguese in the sugar trade. The sixth wave reflected British innovations: the cultivation of Virginia tobacco and the Molasses-Slaves-Rum triangular trade. During the seventh wave the previous luxury products, coffee, sugar and tea, were imported in sufficient quantity to become staples. The beginnings of the Industrial Revolution also occurred during the seventh wave. This wave corresponds to what I called the agriculture/commerce economy in the US. The next three waves are the cotton/textile, railroad/industrial and mass-market economies in the US that I have already discussed. The U.S. information economy is the eleventh wave since the 15th century.

Table 6.4 compares the maturity booms for the innovation waves/leading sectors with Kondratiev upwaves. For the pre-1800 waves, the period from the 50% extent level to the economic peak was used as the maturity boom. With one exception, there is a one-to-one correspondence between upwaves and maturity booms. The average length of the maturity booms of 27 years is quite close to the 25-year average length of the upwaves. Maturity booms overlap with upwaves to an extent far beyond what one would expect from chance. Table 6.4 shows the difference between the beginning of the maturity boom and the K-trough in terms of longwave cycle length at that time. The difference between the economic peak and the K-peak is shown as well. If there were no correspondence between the maturity boom and the upwave we should expect these differences to range between zero and one-half a cycle, with an average of about one-quarter of a cycle. The magnitude of the differences shown in Table 6.4 ranges from zero to 0.41, with an average value of 0.13, considerably less than 0.25. We can look into the probability of the pattern seen by noting how many of the upwave-maturity date differences are above the expected average value of one-quarter cycle. There are five differences that are either close to 0.25 or above, which are denoted in italics in Table 6.4. For there to be no real correlation between maturity booms and upwaves, we would have to assume that the five above average and fifteen below average differences occurred by random chance. This is analogous to flipping 20 coins and getting fifteen or more heads. Referring to the binomial distribution (see chapter two) we find the probability of such an event is 0.6%. This means that it is more than 99% likely that the correspondence suggested by Table 6.4 is real.

Table 6.4 Leading Sector Maturity Booms Compared to Kondratiev Upwaves

Leading Sector / "New" Economy	Maturity Booms	Upwaves	Difference (cycles)	
Portuguese Guinea Gold	1480-1495	1460*-1483	0.41	0.32
	--	1509-1528		
Portuguese Indian Pepper/Spanish American Gold	1540-1555	1538-1557	0.07	0.06
Span Silver/Dutch Baltic Trade/Port Sugar & Asian Trade	1565-1600	1571-1597	0.17	0.08
Dutch Asian Trade	1620-1665	1621-1650	0.02	0.25
British & Dutch Indian Textiles / Dutch Sugar	1695-1725	1689-1711	0.11	0.22
British Rum, Slaves & Tobacco	1726-1767	1738-1767	0.24	0
British Coffee, Sugar & Tea; US Agriculture/Commerce	1786-1802	1789-1813	0.06	0.24
US Cotton / Textile	1843-1861	1843-1864	0	0.06
US Railroad / Industrial	1895-1917	1897-1919	0.04	0.04
US Mass-market	1944-1973	1949-1980	0.10	0.11
Average Length	**27**	**25**	**0.12**	**0.15**

*Value for K-trough from Braudel[27]

Of course, the industries included in each leading sector were chosen as examples of economic activity for particular historical periods. Unlike the examples for the mass-market or railroad/industrial economy, in which many series were combined to form a composite, many of the waves in Figure 6.10 have just one data series in them. Since the source for several of these series is Modelski's book it is not surprising that the sectors should line up with the longwave as Modelski found. Modelski looked at peaks in growth rates, however, rather than looking at the maximum economic extent as I do. His peaks are different from mine and correlate with the mid-point of the downwave (or growth boom peaks), not to K-peaks as do mine. Nevertheless, with my different methodology results strongly supporting Modelski's leading sector model were obtained. Also, it is a historical fact that the Portuguese reached Guinea in the mid-15th century; Vasco de Gama reached India and Columbus discovered the new world in the 1490's; and the Spanish conquered Peru and secured Potosi silver around 1540. All three events are spaced about 50 years (one longwave cycle) apart The growth of the economic activities made possible by these discoveries will also necessarily be spaced one longwave cycle apart.

Similarly, British colonization of the New World was lagged by three cycles over that of Spain. The first permanent Spanish New World colonies were established by Columbus during the first cycle downwave (1483-1509). In contrast, the first British colonies were founded during the fourth downwave (1597-1621). The peak in the Spanish silver economy occurred around the fourth K-peak. The British tobacco, slave and rum economy peaked near the seventh K-peak, three cycles later.

Modelski's leading sector concept[25] and Goldstein's comprehensive summary of the longwave[17] provide a substantial body of evidence for the existence of the longwave as both a real and repetitious economic phenomenon. The development of the Internet or information economy today certainly appears to be yet another one of these leading sectors and was identified as such by longwave scholars as early as the late 1970's.[23,25] The appearance of a new economy can be taken as evidence for the continued operation of the longwave. Thus, rather than invalidating the historical thesis presented here, the recent appearance of the "Internet economy" supports it.

Schumpeter's Innovation Theories

Schumpeter developed a theory[22] in which the innovation wave served as the cause of the longwave. During the late downwave (what Dent calls the shakeout) there is a period of entrepreneurial innovations which serve as the basis for the new economy to come. After the K-trough these new innovative industries start their growth phase. The first part of the growth phase is called the primary wave and it is typified by explosive growth in the new industries. The new industries are still small at this time though, so in absolute terms, most economic growth is due to the mature growth of established industries, which are in their maturity boom. Schumpeter describes the leaders of these industries as the "old men". In the period leading up to the K-peak, the mature businesses of the old men (i.e. the old economy) reaches its limits to growth.

A bout of inflation occurs (often associated with a "peak war") and in its aftermath the economy falls into the primary recession.

After the primary recession a new growth period begins, called the secondary wave. This period is typified by the rise to prominence of "new men", who represent the new economy. By this time (late growth boom) the new economy has grown to a point where its still-rapid growth is large enough to more than counteract the decline in the old, and the overall economy surges ahead. This period is also a time of massive speculation in the new enterprises. At some point, debt levels and investment valuations reach an unsustainable level and the invest-ment-led boom ends. This period is followed by the secondary reces-sion, which lasts to the K-trough. During this period, the new economy consolidates and develops a set of mature innovations that will help drive its growth during the forthcoming maturity boom. At the same time, the basic innovations that will lead to the primary growth phase of the next economy are taking place (see Figure 6.5).

Table 6.5. Schumpeter's innovation-based model for the longwave

Period	Old Economy	New Economy
DG-peak to K-trough	mature innovations & consolidation	basic innovations
Upwave	mature growth, "old men"	primary wave
Region around K-peak	limits of growth, primary recession	
K-peak to DG peak	decline of the "old men"	secondary wave, "new men"
DG-peak to K-trough		mature innovations & consolidation

Schumpeter sees innovation as being particularly enhanced during hard times (necessity is the mother of invention). Two kinds occur, mature and basic innovations, although Schumpeter is mostly con-cerned with the latter. So we have the early development of the railroad occurring during the late downwave of the first U.S. longwave cycle (around the time of the cotton/textile shakeout). There was also the development of the clipper ship and McCormick's reaper (both mature innovations) during this same time. During the late downwave of the second U.S. longwave cycle, there were the key basic innovations of electricity and the automobile, which powered the development of the mass-market economy. At the same time there were mature innovations such as the development of the refrigerator railroad car that permitted shipment of perishables from the Midwest to East Coast consumers.

The late downwave of the third U.S. longwave cycle was once again a hotbed of innovation, e.g. television, electronic computers, plastics, and antibiotics. But in this case, almost all of the innovations were adopted by established business as maturity innovations, even startling new technologies like computers, which in past cycles would have launched new entrepreneurial industries. There were a few new basic innovations such as fast food (McDonalds, KFC) and instant photography (Polaroid). This aggressive adoption of the new by existing businesses showed that the "old men" of the third longwave cycle had learned from their predecessors in the previous waves. As a result, the maturity boom following the third K-trough in 1949 was a particularly strong one, while the primary wave was unusually weak. Not surprisingly, when the mass-market economy finally reached its limits to growth in 1973, there were only a few "new men" (e.g. Perot, Kroc, Land), not nearly enough to take the reins from the old and establish a new economy. But in time reinforcements would come, and with them, the new information economy.

The delayed information economy and lengthened fourth US longwave

During the late downwave of the third cycle and the upwave of the fourth, far-sighted U.S. statesmen saw how the government could intervene in the economy, to help promote growth and moderate the fluctuations. Seeing how innovations were the driver of economic growth, educational programs like the GI bill (1944) which encouraged college attendance were created. Like always, the postwar upwave was a time of destructive "hot wars" (Korea, Vietnam). But there were also other non-destructive "wars" (e.g. Cold War, Space Race, War on Poverty, War on Cancer). Each in turn produced important inputs into the future Information Economy: Cold War information technology (including the Internet), the post-Sputnik National Defense Education Act of 1958, the Higher Education Act of 1965 from the War on Poverty, and the development of genetic engineering from the War on Cancer. As a result of these government initiatives, the innovation period for a new economy occurred during an upwave.

Despite all the government help, it still takes time to breed a new economy. Hence the Information Economy with its "new men" was not yet ready in 1973 when the mass-market economy peaked (Bill Gates was still a teenager). As a result, the economy remained in a stagflation mode until Paul Volcker crushed inflation by inducing the most severe recession since the Depression. It wasn't until after the 1990 recession that the secondary wave came into full swing and the new men (e.g. Gates of Microsoft, Groves of Intel, Case of AOL, Bezos of Amazon.com) rose to prominence. So it seems that the information economy is following the mass production economy by about 70 years, rather than ~53 years, implying that the information economy arrived as much as 17 years "late" relative to previous new economies. In previous cycles, the growth boom of the next economy started 15, 14, and 9 years before the economic peak. Extrapolation of this trend suggests that the next growth boom should have started about seven years before the economic peak in 1973 instead of eight years afterward. So it would appear that the information economy started 15-17 years late.

As suggested above, the delay in arrival of the information growth boom seems to have delayed the K-peak. Just one year after the mass-market peak there was a peak in producer price inflation rates that some researchers denote as the K-peak rather than 1980, as I have done here. But at the three previous K-peaks, the economy was well into the growth boom of the next economy. With no new economy to pick up the slack, the old economy soldiered on, operating at its limits and producing stagflation. Inflation did not finally decline until after 1980, making 1980 the most sensible choice of the K-peak. The delay in K-peak to 1980 resulted in a longwave cycle of 61 years, 8 years longer than average, which reduced the "lateness" of the innovation wave relative to the long-wave to only 7-9 years.

A question naturally arises, will the longwave lengthen still more during the downwave in order to allow the innovation wave to "catch up", or will the progress of the innovation wave be faster this cycle? If one projects the composite growth curve in Figure 6.9 to 90-100% extent, one obtains an estimate of 2007 for the end of the growth boom. Adding the seven year average length of the shakeout to this figure yields an estimate of 2014 for the K-trough using innovation criteria. In contrast, extrapolation of the longwave in the previous chapter suggested 2010-13 as the K-trough, implying some additional lengthening of the cycle may occur.

Summary and Discussion of Findings

In this chapter we explored the idea, first put forth by Schumpeter, that economic development over time can be described as a succession of new economies that appear with a Kondratiev periodicity. We carefully assigned dates to Dent's four stages of the innovation wave. We interpreted the new Internet economy of today as merely the fourth such economy in the US since the late 18th century. Or, in Modelski's terminology, it is the eleventh new leading sector since the 15th century. New economies are a recurring phenomenon and constitute nothing new; they have appeared in the past and secular bear markets still happened. In short, the Internet is just the latest in as series of "new" economies and not the start of a totally new era.

We noted an apparent lengthening of the longwave from the third to fourth US cycle that might reflect a delay in the establishment of a new economy. We advanced the idea that the delay might reflect the time necessary for accumulation of sufficient basic knowledge for exploitation by the information economy innovators, since the basic innovations of the previous downwave had largely been appropriated as maturity innovations. Another possibility is that improved management of the economy by the financial authorities has resulted in a delaying effect on the progression of the longwave.

We projected the end of the growth boom around 2007 and end of the shakeout around 2014. The 2007 date is consistent with Dent's own projection, which is based on an entirely different criterion. Based on the analysis of the longwave in the previous chapter we put the end of the secular bull market around 2000-2004, up to seven years before the end of the growth boom. I note that the postwar secular bull market ended seven years before the mass-market maturity boom peak. Going back we note that the New Era secular bull market (1921-29) ended eight years before the mass-market growth boom peak and the Civil War secular bull market (1861-81) ended seven years before the railroad/industrial growth boom peak. So an estimate of 2000-4 for the end of the current secular bull market is quite consistent with a growth boom peak in 2007.

Here is where we part company with Dent. Dent believes that the economy and market will stay strong until the end of the growth boom. Only after this date will the economy fall into a slump and a secular bear market develop. Dent did not analyze the innovation waves using S-curve analysis like we have here. He assumes that previous growth and maturity booms ended at about the same time as their respective bull markets did. He relates the innovation wave to a generation type and a demographic construct he calls the spending wave (see chapter seven) and uses these to determine dates. The current growth boom is associated with the spending power of the largest generation ever, the baby boomers. Similarly the postwar maturity boom was associated with the spending power of what Dent calls "the Bob Hope generation".

Before that, the mass-market growth boom was associated with the spending power of the "the Henry Ford generation".

Dent's generations come from a fascinating book called *Generations* by Neil Howe and William Strauss.[28] Using the generation scheme provided by these authors along with Dent's economic interpretation gives 2006 as the end of the current growth boom. Application of the spending wave gives 2007. This is the source of Dent's 2007 projection. Moving back, the generational criterion gives 1969 as the end of the last maturity boom, whereas the spending wave gives 1966, which agrees very well with the broad top of the postwar secular bull market over 1966-1972. For the previous growth boom, the generation criterion gives 1927 and the spending wave gives 1929 as the end, which agrees well with the market peak in 1929.

The excellent correspondence between generations and the spending wave breaks down before 1929. Based on the spending wave the railroad maturity boom should have ended around 1907, while the generation criterion would have no railroad maturity boom at all! The generation criterion applied to the railroad growth boom would have it end in 1866, whereas the spending wave gives 1880. Dent's alignment of generations and the spending wave with his phases of the innovation wave seems to break down after going back more than one cycle. In contrast, the longwave seems to have "worked" tolerably well for ten cycles.

Taken together, the bearish interpretation of the stock cycle, the longwave and the innovation wave presented here fit the facts best. In the next chapter, we take stock of our findings and consider the arguments of the bulls.

Chapter Seven

A Recap and
the Bullish Response

A lot of information has been presented in the last five chapters. In this chapter, this information and the conclusions drawn from it are summarized. After this, a number of arguments that counter these conclusions will be presented. At the end it will be left to the reader to decide for herself the best approach to take with regard to her investments, but at least she will have an understanding of the assumptions she will be making with that choice.

Chapter One: Introduction

The problem with predictions based on historical patterns was presented. Although highly successful predictions have been achieved using these methods (e.g. the calendar), more often predictions are unsuccessful (e.g. astrology).

Chapter Two: Historical Stock Market Performance

We considered the problem of figuring out whether to invest one's 401K money in a money market or S&P500 stock index fund. The historical record was consulted and it showed that if valuation still matters, a money market is the better investment. If "things are different now" then we should ignore valuation and stay in stocks.

Chapter Three: Stock Market Cycles

The concept of secular bull and bear markets was introduced, which together constitute the stock cycle. The price to resources ratio (P/R) was identified as a marker for the stock cycle. It was also shown to be a good indicator of historical valuation and was the tool used to select overvalued markets in chapter two. It was shown that variable perform-ance over time is due to the stock cycle and that strings of good years (like now) naturally occur and are eventually followed by strings of bad years. This says the excellent performance of the past 17 years is in itself a reason to believe the performance over the next 10-20 years will be bad. The counter argument is that because the market has gone up for so much longer than anyone believed to be possible, something *must* be different now and history no longer applies. To address this issue we needed to look deeper to see what causes the stock cycles.

Chapter Four: Understanding Stock Market Behavior

Here we learned that the stock cycles reflect changes in the monetary environment (inflation and interest rates) and in real economic growth. Low inflation rates and long periods of steady economic growth are good for stocks; the converse are not. A model was developed that shows that today's excellent stock performance and high valuations are consistent with historical valuations once the length of modern eco-nomic expansions are taken into account. As long as steady earnings growth continues, (i.e. we don't have a recession) and inflation stays tame, stocks should keep rising. This finding is important because it says that high valuations do not represent some new way of thinking about stocks. More importantly, it says that if the two economic drivers for the bull market (steady growth and low inflation) ever change for the worse, old-style valuations would come back and a major drop in the S&P500 index would be the likely result.

Chapter Five: The Kondratiev Cycle

Having determined that the remarkable stock market performance of recent years reflects remarkably persistent noninflationary economic growth, we need to learn whether this sort of economic nirvana has occurred before, and if so, what was the aftermath? We learned that the inflationary characteristics of the economy vary with a 53-odd year periodicity, that is called the Kondratiev cycle or longwave. The Kondratiev cycle also shows up in the GDP and in the stock cycles, although there are two of each of these per Kondratiev. We found that the period corresponding to today contains the period with the best peacetime economic growth of each cycle, and that this period will likely end within a few years.

After this wonderful economic period, according to my interpretation of the longwave, a secular bear market will begin giving rise to the sort of poor stock returns forecast in chapter two. This explanation does not address the phenomenon of the Internet, which the bulls say changes everything about the economy, and so justifies a continued bull market.

Chapter Six: The Innovation Wave

To address this "Internet issue" we looked at how periodic waves of innovations produce successive new economies that appear with Kondratiev frequency. The information economy much discussed today is the fourth new economy for the US and is associated with the fourth Kondratiev longwave. Alternately, it can be interpreted as the eleventh leading sector of the world economy since the 15th century. Rather than invalidating longwave analysis, the appearance of the new Internet economy at this point in history strengthens the idea that a longwave is still operative and that a secular bear market is imminent. At this point we finally have obtained enough information to conclude:

1. There is a longwave phenomenon in the economy that produces new economies like today's net economy; i.e. the Internet is nothing new and it *should* be happening now.
2. In the past this same cycle has produced both inflationary and recessionary episodes with their associated bear markets. The changing character of the economy as it progresses through the Kondratiev cycle causes the stock market cycles.
3. Application of cycle analysis to the current cycle indicates the start of a recessionary secular bear market in 1999±5, the DG economic peak in 2001±4 and the DG inflation peak in 2002±4.
4. This finding is in agreement with the independent forecast made in chapter three that made use of P/R.

Nagging Concerns

There are still some problems, and they are difficult ones. If this wave is so fundamental to our economy, how come it is not better known and taught in our schools? All of the information on the longwave I have presented has been studied by economic historians, political scientists and sociologists. Researchers have been all over this territory and there is still no consensus amongst scholars that a longwave even exists as a real phenomenon, much less that one can make any sort of predictions using it. A number of possible causes have been advanced for the long-wave (I described one of these). None of them have been accepted universally by longwave scholars. If a sufficiently detailed mechanism could be found, perhaps a predictive model could be built by economists and its predictions checked against reality. In a way, this book represents a test of the longwave by making a specific prediction that a noninflationary secular bear market will start between 2000 and 2004 and last at least until 2010, and quite probably, longer.

Correlation is not the same as causation. The simple observation that B has followed A in the past does not mean that the next time we see A,

B will necessarily follow. However, repeated observations of B following A makes it more likely. The astronomers who developed the calendar had no mechanism, just repeated correlation, and they were right. On the other hand, the astrologers, lacking a mechanism, and having far fewer accurate correlations, were wrong. The observation of the long-wave is necessarily subjective. Which price peaks are labeled as K-peaks, and which industries are chosen to represent a new economy/leading sector? This subjectivity makes the situation seem more similar to astrology than astronomy. Historical cycle research is fraught with pre-dictions of gloom and doom or of a millennium that never seem to come true. It is not surprising that professional social scientists fre-quently take a dim view of the activity.

With a cycle of 50-odd years there has been insufficient time for a lot of cycles to have occurred. Based on the price series, there have been four US K-peaks and K-troughs since 1787 with an average spacing of 54.7±3.8 years. This provides one measure of the longwave cycle length. There have been three innovation waves between 1794 and 1979. If we look at the spacing between successive maturity booms we obtain 53.3±3.4 years as a second estimate for longwave length. Going back before 1787 there is evidence for seven more cycles. Combining all data gives a price cycle of 49±9 years in length and a leading sector cycle of 53±8 years.

There have been seven secular bear and six secular bull markets between 1802 and 1982. The average spacing between secular market peaks and troughs on alternating cycles has been 53±6 years. This pro-vides a third measure of longwave length which is very close to the other two. Not only do these different types of cycles give a similar esti-mate for length, but they line-up together, *just as if they were produced by the same underlying cyclic process.* It is the number and alignment of the cycles that, in my opinion, provides the most compelling evidence for the existence of the longwave. Once we decide that the cycle is real, we do not need a mechanism to use it to make predictions.

The Bullish Case

Here I will present several arguments for why stocks can still go a lot higher. Since the NASDAQ stock market is *still* going up (as of early February 2000) it would seem that this view has a lot of adherents. In the following sections, a number of bullish arguments will be advanced and then critiqued.

Dow 36,000 by James K Glassman and Kevin A Hassett[11]

The authors of *Dow 36,000* argue that stocks are no more risky in the long run than bonds, and that investors are becoming increasingly aware of this fact. They are buying stocks, regardless of price, in lieu of other investments. As a result stock prices rise, reducing the future return of stocks, but providing a one-time windfall gain to those investors astute enough to buy now. They predict that the Dow will rise to about 36,000 over the next five years or so, at which point the future long term return available from stocks will be about the same as that from bonds (about 3% after inflation). They assume a modest 5-6% earnings growth rate in their analysis, which is consistent with long-term growth rates. As a result of this thinking they have proposed that a P/E of 100 is a perfectly reasonable valuation for a large cap index such as the Dow or S&P500.

This argument is self-contradictory. Basically, they argue that since stocks beat bonds over the long term, stocks are no more risky than bonds, and so deserve no risk premium. But it is the risk premium itself that creates the long-term safety of stocks relative to bonds in the first place. Let us measure the risk of stocks relative to bonds as the longest period (T) an investor might have to wait before her stock investment return equals or exceeds the return on bonds. The smaller T is relative to the maturity period for a bond, the safer stocks are relative to bonds.

Stocks become equally safe with bonds when the value T is the same as the maturity period of the bond. We can write:

7.1 $T = \ln(R) / \ln(1+p)$

Here R is the ratio of the highest to lowest market P/E and p is the difference between stock and bond returns. Until recently R has been about 3. The long term real return on stocks in this century has been about 6.8%. The return on AAA-rated corporate bonds has been about 2.4%. This gives p of 4.4%. With these data, equation 7.1 gives an estimate of 25 years for T. We can compare this estimate with the actual historical worst case: buying AAA-rated bonds in 1929 (with interest reinvested in the same) compared to investing in the S&P500 index at the market peak on September 3 (with dividends reinvested). In this case the total return from the stock investment would have overtaken the bond in 1954, 25 years later. So T as calculated by equation 7.1 is a pretty good estimate for stock risk versus bonds.

Now if p were to fall to zero, T becomes infinite and stocks become infinitely risky. Stocks have low risk relative to bonds (as shown by small T relative to a bond maturity) because p is large. In fact, using equation 7.1 we can calculate a level for p of 3.7% associated with equivalent stock risk with the long bond (i.e. when T = 30 years). This value is the same as the risk premium we saw for the 1871-1960 market back in chapter four. It would seem that the market of the past already was pricing stocks more or less equivalently to bonds.

Dow 36,000 makes a "new paradigm" argument for a continued bull market. That is, stocks are priced as high as they are because investors have permanently changed how they look at stocks. As we showed in chapter four, a model can be devised that shows that today's high valuations are completely consistent with decades-old discount-type thinking applied to today's economic reality of a very long expansion with low inflation rate. No new assumptions about investor valuation metrics is necessary to explain recent performance or even much higher levels on the market in the future.

Dow 100,000 Fact or Fiction by Charles W Kadlec[14] and Dow 40000 by David Elias[15]

The authors of these books project that the Dow could reach 40,000 by 2016 (Elias) or 100,000 by 2020 (Kadlec) if the current low-inflation, steady-growth economy continues. As we shown in chapter four, the market model supports these projections given these economic inputs (in fact Elias' estimate is conservative). A 26 (or 30) year economic expansion would be necessary, which these authors maintain is possible because of the enormous markets available through globalization.

These books make a "new era" argument, invoking globalization instead of the Internet as the factor that makes it different this time. All scholars of the longwave agree that the longwave is a global economic phenomenon. Globalization does not negate the longwave, nor the stock cycles that go with it. The Asian crisis and secular downturn in Japan's economy show the global economy of today can still generate events that seem very similar to 19th century panics.

The Roaring 2000's by Harry S. Dent[12]

This book is an update of Dent's earlier book *The Great Boom Ahead*, which forecast that the S&P500 would rise to about 950 (in 1999 dollars) by the year 2007. Dent's predictions are based on his correlation of market performance with a demographic trend he calls the spending wave. The spending wave is simply the birth rate from 44-46 years in the past. The reasoning for its validity is appealing in its simplicity. Since consumer spending rises to a maximum in the mid forties, and consumer spending is the single largest component of GDP, the economy should follow the size of the mid-40's age cohort, which should reflect the birth statistics of some 45 years in the past. Since annual birth data have only been collected since 1909, Dent's analysis starts in the mid-1950's.

In *The Roaring 2000's* Dent presents the same sort of demographic argument, but this time includes immigration data to get a better estimate for the spending wave. He gives the average age of immigrants as 30, which would mean their numbers would swell the size of the age-45 cohort 15 years after their arrival. Dent's revised spending wave is then the sum of the birth rate from ~45 years previously and the immigration rate from 15 years previously. Applying this new method, Dent arrives at a projection of 2900-4400 for the S&P 500 by 2007.

Figure 7.1 shows the spending wave and the real stock index for the period 1865 to 2010. Excellent agreement is seen between the spending wave turning points and those of the stock market after 1920. The spending wave peaked in 1929 and 1966, hitting the ends of the secular bull markets precisely. The spending wave bottomed in 1943 and 1978, in both cases somewhat early.

The spending wave missed the 1906-1921 secular bear market entirely, although it did plateau during the 1907-1919 period. There was a dip between 1880 and 1890, that overlapped the 1881-1896 secular bear market, but the spending wave also was gently rising during the 1870's depression. The record of the spending wave before 1920 is, at best, mixed.

Closer examination of the spending wave shows that about half of its growth for the entire 1943-1966 uptrend occurred before the beginning of the bull market in 1949. During the 1950's, when the market was rising strongly the spending wave was not. If we interpret the spending wave in light of the longwave we see that the spending wave showed strong growth towards the end of the second (1890-1897) and third Kondratiev (1943-1949). The stock market was still in a secular bear market during both of these times. The rise in the spending wave through the next decade may reflect this same tendency.

Figure 7.1 The spending wave versus the constant-dollar stock index

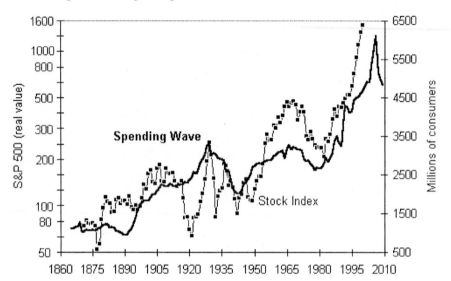

An interesting idea is that the spending wave might act in concert with the longwave, moderating or accentuating its effect. In this view the severity of the 1929 collapse may reflect the combined impact of the longwave fall from plateau and a major decline in the spending wave. In contrast, the severity of the 1990 fall from plateau was ameliorated by the strongly rising trend in the spending wave. If there is anything to this idea it suggests the recession to follow the DG peak may also be another relatively mild event like 1990. As shown in chapter four even a mild recession will produce a severe bear market.

Alternate interpretations of the longwave

If one interprets the inflation peak in 1974 instead of the one in 1980 as the most recent K-peak, one could then assign 1980 as the termination of an upward-sloping plateau instead of a K-peak; the 1986 inflation low as the vortex, and the 1990 inflation peak as the DG peak.[29] Shifting the dates for GDP and the stock index forward in the same way allows us to produce an estimate of 2001±4 for the date of the K-trough for the fourth Kondratiev cycle. In fact, the Asian crisis in 1998 that put in an inflation low of 1.6% and a low in the long bond yield of 4.7% could have been the K-trough. Or, there may be another such crisis in the near future during which even lower lows in inflation and interest rates may be seen, in which case that would be the K-trough.

This interpretation would have the decade since 1990 be the post-DG peak recessionary phase of the downwave, during which the stock market has been in a secular bear market in the last three longwave cycles. In contrast with the previous downwaves, the stock market this time has moved strongly to all-time-highs, and the economy has boomed. In terms of the innovation wave, a 1974 K-peak view would make the Internet either a maturity type innovation for the PC (like television was for radio) or a new basic innovation to be rolled out in the coming primary wave. The shakeout would be occurring right now and is manifested by the declining valuations on old-economy companies and the rising valuations on new-economy companies. Over the next few years the old and new economy will consolidate and after that, a new upwave begin. Strong earnings growth and generally rising markets in stocks and commodities would then ensue with the next major secular bear market to occur during the period leading up to the new K-peak in around 2025. Hence the outlandish valuations on stocks today, especially the "new economy stocks" reflects anticipation of the imminent upwave. Eric von Baranov, a proponent of this view expresses it this way:[30]

> In many cases the psychology that is needed to profit from and comprehend this period borders on fantasy. Without the leap of faith and the anticipation of massive growth the transition period is confusing and difficult to manage.

Prior to the present cycle each long wave contained two secular bull markets, during which returns averaged 13.2% after inflation, and two secular bear markets with an average real return of 0.3% for an average return of 6.8% for the entire cycle. The bullish 1974-as-K-peak interpretation of the longwave implies that there is now only one secular bear market per cycle, the inflationary one. About three quarters of the time the market is in a secular bull market giving the 13% real return and one quarter of the time it is in a secular bear market giving essentially no return, for an average of about 9% over the entire cycle. This is a third higher than the past.

During the 50 years of the current longwave cycle, dividends have averaged 3.7% and real earnings have grown at a 3% rate. Assuming a constant P/E stock prices would have risen at a 3% real rate, which, with the addition of dividends, gives the a long-term real return on stocks of 6.7%, close to the 200 year average. In actual fact, stocks have returned more than 9% in real terms over this period, with the discrepancy caused by the quadrupling of P/E. My interpretation of the longwave holds that the K-trough is still a decade or more away, during which time stocks will provide little, or quite possibly, a negative real return. By the time the cycle ends, the total return on stocks for the entire cycle will be close to the 200 year average of 6.8%. In contrast, the bullish interpretation of the longwave holds that long-term returns have now moved up to the 9% level, implying that a quadrupling of the market multiple should occur every cycle. In this sense the bullish view on the longwave becomes another new paradigm argument, like the Dow 36,000 argument discussed above.

What to make of it all?

We see in this chapter that there is a lot of disagreement with the bearish story developed over the past five chapters. There is the question of whether longwaves even exist. In addition there are a number of arguments that suggest why it could be different this time. The principle reason for my bearish conclusions on the market is its consistency with what has happened before. The view taken here assumes that the stock market will continue to function in the same way, delivering the same long term real return of just under 7% that it always has. I propose that the stock market and economy will follow the same longwave timetable and do the same basic things during each portion of the cycle as they have in the past. The details will be different from cycle to cycle (e.g. a great depression following the 1929 fall-from plateau versus a mild recession in 1990), but the themes will be the same.

In contrast, the bullish counterarguments assume that today is special, and represents a departure from the past 200 years of US economic history. The principal reason for these arguments is the extraordinary performance of the stock market since 1997. The nearly 250% gain in the NASDAQ index in the 17 months after October 1998 is unprecedented on a major index. Clearly, either something truly epoch-making is underway, or the NASDAQ is in a bubble. A bubble occurs when asset values rise beyond all rational assessment of their value as demonstrated by a subsequent collapse in price.

Figure 7.2 shows a graph of the British stock index during the first half of the 18th century. Also shown is the interest rate on government bonds and the same stock index adjusted for the effect of interest rates on stock valuations. There were very few stocks in London stock market at this time. The spike in 1720, was largely the product of a single company, the South Sea Company, and a number of high-flying imitators for which the term "bubble" was originally coined. For this reason it is known as the South Sea bubble.[31] It is one of the most famous episodes of speculative excess, along with the Dutch tulip mania of the 1630's. The peak reached in 1720 was not exceeded for 150 years, clearly making the episode a bubble.

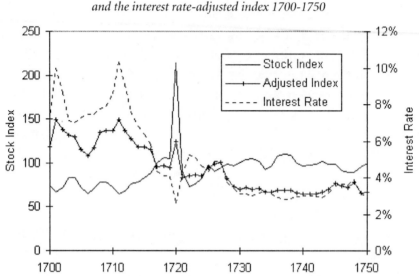

Figure 7.2. British stock index, interest rates, and the interest rate-adjusted index 1700-1750

When the bubble collapsed thousands of British citizens were ruined, including Sir Isaac Newton. If the Master of the Mint (no stranger to matters financial) who was also a genius participated, how irrational was participation in the bubble? Consider, on an interest-adjusted basis stocks were 17% *cheaper* in 1720 than they had been in 1711. A reasonable argument could be made that shares in 1720 were fairly valued relative to their *future* income, just as is argued today about Internet stocks.

So the question becomes, does the extraordinary performance of the NASDAQ today reflect a fundamental change in the world of economics and finance or is it a bubble? If my thesis that nothing fundamental has changed is correct, then the future returns on the stock market are predicted to be poor, and the NASDAQ is in a bubble.

The next and final chapter contains a discussion of what to expect in the forthcoming secular bear market. The historical record will again be consulted to provide guidance as to when one might start moving back into index funds, and what other sorts of investments might be attractive.

Chapter Eight

How to Deal with a Secular Bear Market

In this chapter we assume that the thesis developed in the preceding six chapters is correct, that a secular bear market is coming and that the most likely returns on a stock index fund over the next 5, 10, or 20 years will be poor. The perspective taken will be that of an ordinary person deciding what sort of mixture of funds she should employ in her 401K to maximize her chances of getting an adequate return over the next decade or two.

As a market historian I can tell you what sorts of assets did well at various times, but I lack the training to make specific recommendations. My view on this topic is if you know enough to be handling your own investments you will know what to do with the information in this book. If you are unsure on how to proceed then consult a financial advisor. Simply have them read this book and ask them to recommend an asset allocation mix based on it. He or she will be able to recommend a mixture of assets that will be able to deal with the "financial weather" associated with the seasons of the longwave cycle.

Financial advisors use the term *asset allocation* to describe this mixture. The idea is to have some of each kind of asset so that the portfolio of assets grows at a reasonably steady rate over the long term. Since different asset types perform well under different conditions a mix of all major types should have one class doing well at all time.

There are two basic approaches to asset allocation, static and dynamic. Static allocation uses a fixed percentage in each asset class. An example of a fixed allocation is Harry Browne's Permanent Portfolio.[32]

Brown advocates putting 25% of your assets in each of four asset classes: stocks (an index fund), bonds (a US government bond fund), cash (a money market fund) and gold. Such a portfolio has provided a fairly steady return over the long haul. It suffers from the disadvantage that several of its asset classes can do extremely poorly for extended periods of time. Gold has done very poorly over the last 17 years, while stocks have done extremely well. Conversely, gold did well in the 1970's inflation while bonds did horribly and stocks were pretty lousy too. A static allocation is employed when one believes that the markets are so random that it is unwise to make any guesses as to which asset classes might be favored at certain times.

Dynamic allocation uses a variable percentage of various asset classes. The amount of each kind of asset is varied depending on the investor's view of the relative attractiveness of an asset type. To practice dynamic asset allocation one needs to have some sort of view of what lies ahead in the financial markets. The objective would be to over-weight one's allocation towards the types of assets that will do well in the coming years and to underweight the allocation towards asset types expected to do less well. The first thing we note is that since stocks out-perform all other types of assets in the long run, our portfolio should be overweighted in stocks on average over the long run. Over the long run bonds outperform cash and gold, so on average we should have a larger allocation towards bonds than these other two assets. Financial profes-sionals typically recommend that an investor keep about 6 months worth of expenses in the form of cash in order to meet unforeseen emergencies. For many people this requirement will take care of the cash allocation.

The concepts of stock and economic cycles discussed in this book lend themselves naturally to the practice of dynamic asset allocation. The example of Mr. A and Ms. B from chapter three shows that, at a minimum, an investor should have half of her assets in stocks on aver-age over the long term. If she is as prescient as Ms. B she could have

100% in stocks during the secular bull markets and 0% in stocks during the secular bear markets. Unfortunately, most of us aren't that good. Using P/R, we can heavily overweight our allocation towards stocks when P/R is at very low levels like it was in the early 1980's. For P/R of 0.5 or less allocation to a stock index of all funds over and above that six month cash reserve would be a very good policy.

Unfortunately, P/R is at record high levels today, suggesting that stocks will give their lowest returns of the cycle over the next decade or so. The question is, what sorts of assets might be preferable to stocks? Table 8.1 shows the projected return on stocks relative to bonds and cash for periods of overvalued stock markets (the same 200 months examined in chapter two is used here). The capital gains data from chapter two (with a small amount of dividends added) was used for the stock returns.

Table 8.1 Return on stocks relative to bonds and cash for overvalued markets

Percentile	vs Bonds (5yr)	vs Cash (5yr)	vs Bonds (10yr)	vs Cash (10yr)
95%	+8.8%	+5.9%	+7.1%	+3.8%
90%	+7.8%	+4.7%	+6.3%	+3.2%
75%	+6.5%	+3.0%	+4.1%	-1.1%
50%	+2.4%	-0.7%	+0.9%	-1.9%
25%	-2.6%	-4.0%	-2.2%	-3.9%
10%	-7.2%	-6.6%	-3.4%	-4.9%
5%	-8.5%	-8.5%	-4.9%	-5.8%
Average	**+1.0%**	**-1.0%**	**+0.8%**	**-1.4%**

We see that cash beats stocks on average over both five and ten year periods. The figures in Table 8.1 differ somewhat from those discussed in chapter one. In that comparison we were comparing the projected stock returns with the *current* yield on money market funds. The results in Table 8.1 use historical real interest rates which, on average, were somewhat lower than they are today. We note that bonds do less well versus stocks than does cash, despite the higher interest rates on bonds. How can this be?

Unlike a money market fund, whose net asset value remains constant, the value of a bond will change with interest rates. When interest rates fall, bond prices rise and a bond fund will yield a total return greater than that obtained from just interest. When interest rates rise, bond prices fall, and a bond fund will yield a total return less than the interest. Recall that there are two kinds of secular bear markets, inflationary and recessionary. Interest rates rise during inflationary periods, and bonds will do worse than cash during inflationary periods. So for half of the secular bear markets, cash is to be preferred over bonds. Many of the entries in Table 8.1 came from the most recent secular bear market, which was inflationary. As a result, the sample of overvalued markets in Table 8.1 is overweighted to pre-inflationary periods and cash comes out looking better than bonds in the comparison.

The coming secular bear market is not going to be of the inflationary variety, if the cyclic analysis presented in the previous chapters is valid. Hence we should restrict our historical examination of stock versus bond performance to just the secular bear markets during the late downwave of the longwave cycle. To do this I selected the periods 1834-1843, 1880-1897 and 1928-1949, which contain the last two years of the preceding disinflationary secular bull market and all of the subsequent recessionary secular bear market. I calculated five year real returns on stocks bonds and cash for all 600 months during these periods. I then ranked them in order of increasing P/R and averaged them in groups of ten. The sixty averages obtained were plotted in Figure 8.1. In general, returns on bonds are better than cash during these low-inflation periods. On average, five year returns on bonds are clearly better than those on stocks when P/R is greater than 0.9. For P/R between 0.5 and 0.9 bonds do about the same or better than stocks. Only for P/R below 0.5 do stocks start to outperform bonds.

Consulting the raw data I can obtain the odds of bonds outperforming stocks as a function of P/R. For P/R of 1.2 and higher (this would roughly correspond to an S&P500 of over 1200 for the next few years) the historical record has both bonds and cash beating stocks 100% of the time over five years. For P/R between 0.9 and 1.2 (corresponding to an S&P500 of about 900-1200 over the next few years) bonds and cash both beat stocks 90% of the time over a five year period. For P/R between 0.5 and 0.9, stocks beat bonds 52% of the time and cash 60% of the time over a five year period. For P/R below 0.5 stocks beat bonds 82% of the time and cash 98% of the time.

Based on these statistics we might recommend a high level of bonds while P/R remains above 0.9, but as it drops below that level a 50:50 mix of stocks and bonds might be better. If P/R falls below 0.5 a high level of stocks is recommended.

Figure 8.1 Real returns (5yr) from different asset types
during recessionary secular bear markets

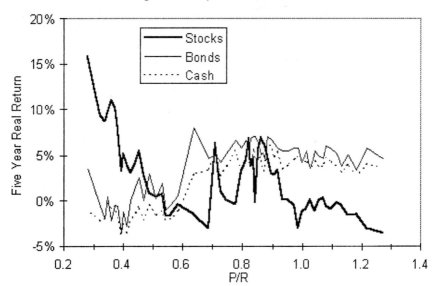

What about gold? Gold is an inflation hedge. It should do well during periods of rising inflation. One might consider gold the "anti-bond". Gold does best when bonds do worst. Thus, a wise choice might be to completely substitute the bond portion of your asset allocation with gold during the period before an inflationary secular bull market, and to not have any gold during the period before a recessionary secular bear market (like now). So I would not recommend gold at this time.

If you are enterprising, the best returns during a recessionary secular bear market would be obtained using the methods of value investing. A few books to get you started are listed here:

1. Benjamin Graham, *The Intelligent Investor*
2. David Dreman, *Contrarian Investment Strategies*
3. Kenneth Lee, *Trouncing the Dow*

Appendix A: Notes

Chapter Two. Construction of the stock index

Historical stock performance data were obtained from an index combining the monthly price indexes of bank stocks[33] (1802-1815), bank and insurance stocks[33] (1815-1845), railroad stocks[33] (1834-1862) and a second index of railroad stocks[34] (1857-1871). For overlapping indices, the average of the monthly changes were calculated and this average used to calculate the change in the composite index. The resulting index for 1802-1871 was spliced onto the Cowles/S&P500 index (1871-present) obtained from Shiller[35,36] Dividends of 6.4% were assumed for the period 1802-1871, based on the average for the 1870's as described by Siegel.[1] Dividends and earnings after 1871 were obtained from Shiller.[35,36] Values were adjusted for inflation using a consumer price index.

This index was constructed by splicing together various consumer price indices in the same way as the stock index. For the period 1802-1820 the PPI series was spliced onto the CPI (see chapter five references). For the period 1820-1960 two series[37,38] were used. A third series provided by Lebergott[39] was added to the other two for the 1860-1946 period. After 1946 government CPI data from the U.S. Department of Labor, Bureau of Labor Statistics was used.[40]

Chapter Three: Calculation of R

For an index, R is given by:

A.1. $\quad R = R_0 + \Sigma (E_i - D_i) \cdot \$CPI_i$

Here E_i and D_i are the earnings and dividend on the index at year i. The parameter $\$CPI_i$ is the value of the historical dollar in year i in terms of 1999 dollars. The parameter R_0 refers to the value of R in a basis year. For the years 1871-1999 values of E_i and D_i were obtained from Shiller.[3] For the years 1802-1871 an estimate was obtained for R using the slope of the stock price trend as a proxy for slope of R as described below.

We define the real earnings (RE) as $E \cdot \$CPI$; the fraction of earnings retained (k) as (E-D) / E. We assume that k is constant. Substituting these into equation A.1 gives:

A.2. $\quad R = R_0 + k \Sigma RE_i$

We can express equation A.2 as an integral:

A.3. $\quad R = R_0 + k \int RE \, dt$

We can write RE as the sum of the value predicted by the real earnings trend RE_T plus a residual value RE_{RES}, defined as the difference between the actual value of RE and RE_T as follows:

A.4. $\quad RE = RE_T + (RE - RE_T) = RE_T + RE_{RES}$

Substituting equation A.4 into equation A.3 yields:

A.5. $R = R_0 + k \int RE_T \, dt + k \int RE_{RES} \, dt$

We propose to calculate RE_T using the real price trend RP_T according to the following relation:

A.6. $RE_T = RP_T / PE_{AVG}$

here PE_{AVG} is the average P/E over the interval, and is assumed to be constant. Combining equations A.5 and A.6 yields:

A.7. $R = R_0 + (k / PE_{AVG}) \int RP_T \, dt + k \int RE_{RES} \, dt$

Now, the integral of E_{RES} should tend to remain bounded as t becomes large, whereas the integral of RP_T should increase without bound. Thus, the ratio of these two integrals should decline with time.

To explore this idea the actual real earnings data for the Cowles index for 1871-1910 are plotted in Figure A.1. Also shown is the earnings trend obtained using the price data and an average P/E of 14.5. Finally RE_{RES} and RP_T/PE_{AVG} were integrated numerically as simple sums and the ratio of the former to the latter plotted in Figure A.1. The figure shows the integral of the residual falling relative to the integral of the trend, just as we would expect.

Figure A.1. Plot of earnings, earnings trend and ratio
of sum of residuals to sum of earnings.

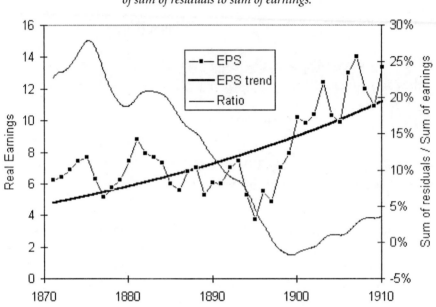

Thus, for fairly lengthy periods of time, we can neglect the second integral in equation A.7 and write:

A.8. $\quad R = R_0 + (k / PE_{AVG}) \int RP_T \, dt$

Now, the price trend RP_T refers to a trend on a semilog plot, meaning that P_T is an exponential function rather than a linear one:

A.9. $\quad RP_T = RP_0 \, e^{rt}$

It then follows that

A.10. $\quad \int RP_T \, dt = (RP_0 / r) \, [e^{rt} - 1] = RP_T / r - RP_0 / r$

Substituting A.10 into A.8 and rearranging yields:

A.11.　　$R - R_0 = [k/(r\,PE_{AVG})]\,RP_T - [k/(r\,PE_{AVG})]\,RP_0$

Comparing similar terms it is evident that:

A.12.　　$R = [k/(r\,PE_{AVG})]\,P_T$

From equation A.12 it is clear that a semilog plot of R will be parallel to a similar plot of the stock price trend. The two parallel lines will be offset by the value $\log[k/(r\,PE_{AVG})]$. A regression line was fit through the market peaks in 1802, 1835, 1852 and 1872 to determine the slope of the trend. Given this slope, a value of R_0 was selected for the year 1802 such that the R projected for the post 1871 period was in line with the values obtained from equation 3.1. R_0 equal to 97% of the 1802 price gave the best fit.

Chapter Four: Development of the modern model of stock market behavior

Unlike bonds, earnings per share and the dividend payments derived from stocks can grow over time. A proper valuation for stocks should consider the anticipated future stream of increasing earnings, with due consideration of the effective interest rate. Valuing a stock on its future earnings makes use of the discount formula:

A.13.　　$P = \Sigma\,E_j/(1+d)^j$　　for $j = 1$ to infinity

Here E_j is the earnings for year j and d is the expected return over time, which is called the discount rate. Although discount-type valuation models were not *explicitly* formulated until the 1930's (and then expressed in terms of dividends rather than earnings), "discount-type thinking" was implicitly operative in the high valuations awarded to stocks as early as the late 1920's.

We can write a special version of equation A.13 by assuming that earnings will grow at two different rates over time. One high rate r_1 extends for n years and is then followed by a much smaller rate r_2 for all time after that. The high rate is larger than d, while the lower rate is lower than d, so that infinite values are not obtained. The expression obtained is:

A.14. $\quad P = E[(1+r_1-d)^n-1]/r_1 + E(1+r_1)^n/(d-r_2)$

To apply this equation we must decide what to use for the initial high growth rate (r_1) and the subsequent low growth rate (r_2). We note that discount-type thinking will only be applied during periods of rising earnings, that is, during economic expansions. During recessions there is no significant earnings growth, in fact, earnings usually contract. Hence, we might designate r_1 as the growth rate in S&P500 earnings during economic expansions (r) and set r_2 equal to zero, to reflect the lack of growth expectations during economic recessions. With these simplifications equation A.14 becomes:

A.15. $\quad P = E[(1+r-i)^n-1]/r + E(1+r)^n/i$

Earnings growth rates during recessions are often (but not always) less than zero. Hence stock investments during recessions are more risky than those made during expansions. A risk premium is in order and we can write:

A.17. $\quad P = E[(1+r-i)^n-1]/r + E(1+r)^n/(i+rp)$

The first term reflects the extra value accorded to stocks by the high levels of growth they are exhibiting now. The second term can be interpreted as the "residual" value stocks will have n years in the future, after the current period of rapid growth is over. At this point, since growth is over, valuation on current earnings is perfectly reasonable. Hence the second term is simply equation 3.3 multiplied by the factor $(1+ r)^n$. That is, it is equation 3.3 applied to earnings n years in the future.

The next step is to determine a value for n. Since earnings growth occurs during economic expansion, it is reasonable to use the length of expansions as n. Figure 4.9 shows a plot of expansion length over time. It is evident that the average length has increased since around the 1920's. Also shown in Figure 4.9 is a moving average of expansion lengths that will be used to provide values for n in the model.

We are now in a position to formally specify the model:

i. $r =$ the larger of: 6.3% or earnings growth over the previous ten years.

ii. $n =$ the average length of economic expansion as defined by figure 4.9

iii. $i =$ effective interest rate

iv. $rp =$ 2.03% risk premium

v. $P_1 =$ $E / (i + rp)$ (Eq. 3.3)

vi. $P_2 =$ $E [(1+ r - i)^n - 1] / r + E (1+ r)^n / (i + rp)$ (Eq. A.18)

vii. $Q =$ sign of the stock index trend over past two years, rising (+) or falling (-)

viii. $P =$ P_1 if Q is negative **or** current index value is less than P_1

ix. $P =$ P_2 if Q is positive **and** current index value is greater than P_1

This model says that the "old" valuation method based on current earnings (P_1) still applies to the modern market *except* when the index moves above P_1 as part of a rising trend. In this case a "new" valuation model (P_2) applies. Qualitatively, what happens is that during a bear market and during the early stages of a bull market, the old model represented by P_1 applies. If the expansion is long enough, the index will move above P_1 and the new valuation model, represented by P_2, applies. This movement above P_1 occurs when the expansion has run long enough to justify starting to incorporate some future into valuations.

Eventually, the expansion comes to an end, and the stock market begins to decline. When the index reaches P_1 or after it has fallen for two years, the old valuation model once again becomes active. The actual output of the stock market model is quite jumpy as it shifts from P_1 to P_2 and back again. A moving average was employed to smooth the model output in Figure 4.10.

Chapter Five: The Kondratiev Cycle

The US producer price series was obtained from Global Financial Data[38] that covered the period from 1720-present. British consumer prices for the 1475-1782 period were obtained from the Brown and Hopkins seven-century series of builder wages and consumer prices.[41-43] For the 1782-1900 period, the index was a composite of the Brown series and a series obtained the OSU Fisher College of Business website.[44] The OSU series was constructed by W. Hoffman from the price data assembled by Lord Beveridge.[45] The producer price index was a composite of four price series: industrial prices[46] (1495-1660); producer prices[47] (1660-1802); wholesale price index[48] (1780-1900); and a commodity price index[49,50] (1750-1900). US interest rates were obtained from Global Financial Data.[38] British interest rates and prices after 1782 were obtained from data series maintained at the OSU Fisher College of Business website.[44] The series was obtained from data assembled by Warren and Pearson (no reference given). U.S. GDP estimates were obtained from a variety of sources. Early data was obtained from a series from Mitchell[51] for the period 1789-1909. Two series, one from

Kendrick[52] and one from the OSU website[44] covered the 1869-1959 period. Data after 1959 was obtained from the Bureau of Economic Analysis.[53] Historical US population was obtained from the Census Bureau.[54]

For Figure 5.1 the producer price index was plotted for the period 1720-1940. For the period 1940-1999, the following expression was plotted:

A.18. $\quad y = 1 + A(x - i_{AVG}); \quad x = (i_{t-1} + 2i_t + i_{t+1})/4$

Here A is an arbitrary parameter, i_t is the consumer price inflation rate for year t and i_{AVG} is the average inflation rate over the 1940-1999 span. Equation A.13 is simply a scaled version of the smoothed inflation rate that can be grafted onto the price plot to give the continuous price/inflation plot shown in Figure 5.1.

Chapter Six. The Innovation Wave

Data were mostly obtained from Mitchell[51] and US Census Statistical Abstracts.[55,56] Semiconductor sales were obtained from the Semiconductor Industry Association.[57] Certain noisy data series were smoothed with a 5-7 year centered moving average, otherwise they were plotted as is. A few series were constructed out of underlying data. Car and Truck output in Figure 6.4 reflects the sum of the output of passenger cars plus 1.4 times the output of commercial vehicles. The 1.4 factor reflects the average ratio of the unit values of commercial vehicles compared to passenger cars. A crude estimate for the total number of appliances was obtained by summing sales over a 15 year moving period. This assumes an average lifetime of 15 years for an appliance. This sum was divided by the labor force to obtain appliances per worker as a measure of market penetration. For the information economy composite wave in Figure 5.9, the ratio of college students to high school students was calculated and 0.38 (the average value in the late 1940's) subtracted from this value. This gives a curve that starts at zero in 1948 and starts to rise in the late 1950's, accelerating in the 1970's and 1980's. This transformation treats the GI bill as the "basic innovation" of college education and so "starts" the S-curve at this point. We then see small increases following the 1958 National Defense Education Act and the 1965 Higher Education Act. Growth becomes endogenous in the mid 1970's and has been growing since.

The data employed for production of the leading sectors was obtained from a number of sources. British Tobacco, Rum, Sugar, Coffee and Tea imports were obtained from Mitchell[51] and Schumpeter.[58] Statistics on the slave trade were obtained from Anstey[59] and Rawley.[60] Spanish silver and gold were obtained from Goldstein,[18] who got them from Hamilton.[61] The rest of the data was from obtained from Modelski.[25] The original sources were: Portuguese gold (Godinho[62]); Portuguese pepper (Mathew[63],Wake[64]); Portuguese Asian Trade (Duncan[65]); Dutch Baltic Shipping (Boswell[66] et al.); Dutch Asian Trade (Steensgaard[67]); Portuguese Sugar (Phillips[68] and Watts[69]); and British and Dutch Indian Trade (Steensgaard[67]).

The leading sector plots for the British Tobacco, Rum & Slave sector, and the Tea, Coffee, and Sugar Sector used trade volumes divided by an estimate of the British GDP trend and so represented "economic penetration" plots. British GDP (after 1830) and population were obtained from Mitchell.[51] Estimates of per capita GDP in 1700, 1750, and 1800 were obtained from Goldstein,[18] based on data from Crafts.[70] Values in between were obtained by log-interpolation, and the results multiplied by population to get an estimate for GDP between 1700 and 1830. Non-British trade data was used in raw form.

Chapter Seven. A Recap and the Bullish Response

I extended Dent's spending wave back before 1953 using two methods. The first method employed Dent's method using a crude estimate for birthrate before 1909 obtained from census data along with the immigration data[71] obtained from the Immigration and Naturalization Service. The second method employed labor force data. I calculated the average rate of labor force increase for sequential 10-year periods. This value reflects the difference in the numbers of young workers entering the work force and old workers leaving it. Because of rapid population growth I assumed that the young workers term dominated and that the change in work force was approximately proportional to the number of workers entering the work force. Assuming an average age of 20 for workforce entrants, this implies that the size of the age 45 cohort should be roughly equal to the number of workforce entrants 25 years earlier (which I assumed was roughly proportional to the change in workforce). Thus, the spending wave is proportional to the change in labor force from 25 years earlier. The labor force-derived values from the 1950's were correlated with the birth-derived[72] values to obtain the proportionality constant, which was then used to calculate the pre-1953 spending wave using labor force data. The two sets of estimates were averaged together to give the pre-1953 spending wave estimate.

References

1. Jeremy Siegel, *Stocks for the long run: the definitive guide to financial market returns and long-term investment strategies*, New York: McGraw-Hill, 1998.

2. Curtis M. Arnold, *Timing the market*, Chicago: Probus Publishing, 1993.

3. J.R. Flynn, (1984) "The mean IQ of Americans: Massive gains 1932 to 1978", *Psychological Bulletin*, **95**, 29-51.

4. J.R. Flynn, (1987) "Massive IQ gains in 14 nations: What IQ tests really measure". *Psychological Bulletin*, **101**, 171-191.

5. J.R. Flynn, "The ontology of intelligence", In *Measurement, Realism and Objectivity*, J. Forge (ed), New York: D. Reidel, 1987, pp 1-40.

6. Robert E. Bronson, Anne E. Yates, "Bronson Asset Allocation Cycles", Bronson Capital Markets Research, Working paper, 1997.

7. Robert E. Bronson, "Price-Earnings Ratios as a Predictor of Future Stock Market Performance", Bronson Capital Markets Research, Working Paper, 1997.

8. Robert Shiller, John W. Campbell, "Valuation Ratios and the Long-Run Stock Market Outlook", *Journal of Portfolio Management* (Winter 1998).

9. Robert Shiller, *Irrational Exuberance*, Princeton NJ: Princeton University Press, 2000.

10. Benjamin Graham, "Stock Market Warning: Danger Ahead", *California Management Review*, 11(3) 1960.

11. James K. Glassman and Kevin A. Hassett, *Dow 36,000: The New Strategy for Profiting From the Coming Rise in the Stock Market*,

12. Harry S. Dent, *The Roaring 2000s: Building the wealth and life style you desire in the greatest boom in history*, New York: Simon and Schuster, 1998.

13. David Elias, *Dow 40,000: strategies for profiting from the greatest bull market in history*, New York: McGraw-Hill, 1999.

14. Charles W. Kadlec, *Dow 100,000 fact or fiction*, New York: New York Institute of Finance, 1999.

15. George Soros, "The alchemy of finance: reading the mind of the market", New York: Simon and Schuster, 1987.

16. Nicolai D. Kondratiev, "The long waves in economic life", (originally published in German, 1926). Translated by W. F. Stolper, *Review of Economic Statistics* 17: 105-115.

17. Joshua S. Goldstein, *Long Cycles*, New Haven: Yale University Press, 1988.

18. Don Roper, *Some Personal Intellectual History To Explain: how I arrived at a monetary interpretation of Kondratieff waves and the choice of 1980, rather than WWII or the Vietnam War, as a turning point* (http://csf.colorado.edu/roper/defl-waves/personal-intellectual-history.html)

19. Brian J. Berry, *Long-wave rhythms in economic development and political behavior*, Baltimore: The Johns Hopkins University Press, 1991.

20. Simon Kuznets, *Secular movements in production and prices: their nature and their bearing upon cyclical fluctuations.* Boston: Houghton Mifflin, 1930.

21. David Knox Barker, *The K-wave: profiting from the cyclical booms and busts in the global economy*, Burr Ridge Illinois: Irwin Professional Publishers, 1995.

22. Joseph A. Schumpeter, *Business Cycles: A theoretical, historical and statistical analysis of the capitalist process.* London: McGraw-Hill, 1939.

23. Gerhard Mensch, *Stalemate in Technology*, Cambridge MA: 1979.

24. Harry S. Dent, *The Great Boom Ahead*, New York: Hyperion 1993.

25. George Modelski and William Thompson, *Leading Sectors and World Powers: The Coevolution of Global Politics and Economics,* University of South Carolina Press, 1996.

26. Paul Kennedy, *The Rise and Fall of the Great Powers,* New York: Vintage Book, 1987.

27. Fernand Braudel, *The Mediterranean and the Mediterranean World in the Age of Philip II,* 1949, reprinted, London: Collins, 1972

28. William Strauss and Neil Howe, *Generations: The History of America's Future 1584 to 2069,* New York: Quill William Morrow 1991.

29. Thomas Drake, Tenerio Research and Trading, personal communication, February 20, 2000.

30. Eric Von Baranov, The Kondratyev Wave Theory Letters, personal communication, February 23, 2000.

31. E. Robert Beckman, *Crashes Why They Happen-What to Do,* London: Sidgwick and Jackson, 1988.

32. Harry Browne, *Why the Best-Laid Investment Plans Usually Go Wrong,* New York: William Morrow and Co., 1987.

33. Walter B. Smith and Arthur H. Cole, *Fluctuations in American Business,* New York: Russell & Russell, 1935, p 173-184.

34. Frederick R. Macauley, *Some Theoretical Problems suggested by the Movements of Interest Rates, Bond Yields and Stock Prices in the United States Since 1856*, New York: National Bureau of Economic Research, 1938, A142-A161.

35. Robert Shiller (www.econ.yale.edu/~shiller/chapt26.html)

36. Robert J. Shiller, *Market Volatility*, MIT Press, MIT Press, 1989.

37. Robert Sahl, Oregon State University (www.orst.edu /Dept/pol_sci/ sahr/cpi96.htm)

38. Global Financial Data (www.globalfindata.com)

39. Stanley Lebergott, *Manpower in Economic Growth, The American Experience Since 1800*, NewYork: McGraw-Hill 1964.

40. Federal Reserve Bank of St. Louis (www.stls.frb.org/fred/data/ cpi/cpiaucns)

41. E. H. Phelps Brown and Sheila V. Hopkins, "Builders' Wage-rates, Prices and Population: Some Further Evidence," Economica (February 1959): 18-37

42. E. H. Phelps Brown and Sheila V. Hopkins, "Seven Centuries of the Price of Consumables, compared with Builders' Wage-rates," Economica (November 1956): 296-314.

43. E. H. Phelps Brown and Sheila V. Hopkins, "Wage-rates and Prices: Evidence for Population Pressure in the Sixteenth Century," Economica (November 1957): 289-306

44. Ohio State University, Fisher College of Business (www.cob.ohio-state.edu/~fin/ resources_data/data)

45. Lord Beveridge, *Prices and Wages in England from the Twelfth to Nineteenth Century*, Vol. 1 1939, reprinted, New York: Augustus M. Kelly, 1966.

46. Peter H. Ramsey, *The Price Revolution in Sixteenth Century England*, London: Methuen, 1971.

47. Elizabeth Schumpeter (1938) "English Prices and Public Finance 1660-1822", *Review of Economic Statistics*, **20**: 21-37.

48. B. R. Mitchell, *British Historical Statistics*, Cambridge University Press, 1988.

49. Nikolai Kondratiev, "Dynamics of Industrial and Agricultural Prices", *Economic Bulletin of the Conjuncture Institute*, 1928.

50. Jacob J. van Duijn, *The Long Wave in Economic Life*, London: George Allen and Unwin, 1983.

51. B. P. Mitchell, *International Historical Statistics: The Americas 1750-1993*, New York: Stockton Press, 1998.

52. John W. Kendrick, *Productivity Trends in the United States*, National Bureau of Economic Research No. 71, Princeton University Press 1961.

53. US Department of Commerce, Bureau of Economic Analysis, National Accounts Data webpage (www.bea.doc.gov/bea/dn1.htm)

54. US Department of Commerce, Bureau of the Census (www.census.gov).

55. United States Department of Commerce, Bureau of the Census, *Historical Statistics of the United States from Colonial Times to 1970*, U.S. Government Printing Office, 1975.

56. United States Department of Commerce, Bureau of the Census, *Statistical Abstract of the United States,* U.S. Government Printing Office, various years from 1990-1998.

57. Semiconductor Industry Association (www.semichips.org)

58. Elizabeth B. Schumpeter, *English Overseas Trade Statistics*, 1697-1808, Oxford: Clarendon Press, 1960.

59. Roger Anstey, *The Atlantic slave trade and British abolition, 1760-1810*, Atlantic Highlands NJ: Humanities Press, 1975.

60. James A. Rawley, *The Transatlantic Slave Trade: A History*, New York: Norton, 1981.

61. Earl J. Hamilton, *American Treasure and the Price Revolution in Spain*, Cambridge MA: Harvard University Press, 1934.

62. V.M. Godinho, *Os Discombrimentos e a Economia Mundial,* Lisboa: Editorial Presencias, 1963-65.

63. K. S. Matthew, *Portuguese Trade with India in the Sixteenth Century*, New Delhi: Manchar, 1983.

64. C. H. H. Wake (1979) "The Changing Pattern of Europe's Pepper and Spice Imports, ca. 1400-1700", *Journal of European Economic History*, 8: 361-403.

65. T. Bentley Duncan, "Navigation Between Portugal and Asia in the Sixteenth and Seventeenth Centuries", In Cyriac K. Pullapilly and Edwin J. Van Kley, eds., *Asia and the West: Encounters and Exchanges from the Age of Explorations*, Notre Dame IN: Cross Cultural Publications, 1986.

66. Terry Boswell, J. Misra, and J Brueggemann, "The Rise and Fall of Amsterdam and Dutch Hegemony: Evidence for the Baltic Sound Tolls, 1550-1750". In R. Kasaba ed., *Cities in the World-System*, New York: Greenwood, 1991.

67. Nels Steengaard, "The Growth and Composition of the Long Distance Trade of England and the Dutch Republic Before 1750". In James D. Tracey, ed., *The Rise of the Merchant Empires: Long Distance Trade in the Early Modern World 1350-1750*, Cambridge: Cambridge University Press, 1990.

68. Carla R. Phillips, "The Growth and Composition of Trade in the Iberian Empires, 1450-1750", In James D. Tracey, ed., *The Rise of the Merchant Empires: Long Distance Trade in the Early Modern World 1350-1750*, Cambridge: Cambridge University Press, 1990.

69. David Watts, *The West Indies: Patterns of Development, Culture and Environmental Change Since 1492*, Cambridge: Cambridge University Press, 1987.

70. N. F. R. Crafts (1983) "Gross National Product in Europe, 1870-1910: Some New Estimates", *Explorations in Economic History*, **20**: 387-401.

71. U.S. Immigration and Naturalization Service, *Statistical Yearbook of the Immigration and Naturalization Service, 1994*, U.S. Government Printing Office: Washington, D.C., 1996.

72. Center for Disease Control, National Center for Health Statistics (www.cdc.gov/nchs/)

About the Author

Michael Alexander Ph.D. is a research engineer at Pharmacia Corporation. He has had a lifelong interest in economic and stock market history. Stock Cycles is the result of five years of research and is his first book. He resides in Kalamazoo MI.

If you enjoyed *Stock Cycles*,
check out this iUniverse title:

Dale R. Geiger
Winning the Cost War
Applying Battlefield Management Doctrine
to the Management of Government

"**Winning the Cost War** has moved managerial costing
from being a secondary chore to a framework for success
in today's environment. A must-read for agency and
corporate leaders who need to adopt battlefield instincts of
strategy and tactics and apply them in the new fiscal war."
--Ward Melhuish, partner, PricewaterhouseCoopers LLP

As the United States moves from Cold War to Cost War,
the management of cost has greatly increased in
importance. In fact, the greatest threat today to the
strength of the nation may be poor management of the
limited remaining resources.

Winning the Cost War documents a new doctrine of cost
management developed from battlefield management, one
of management's oldest applications. Dale Geiger defines
and illustrates new ideas for everything from managerial
cost accounting to analysis and accountability.

Available through your local bookstore
or at www.iuniverse.com.

Printed in the United States
1203900001B/392